C000242140

A Dictionary of BOMBER COMMAND 1939-1945

A Dictionary of BOMBER COMMAND 1939-1945

GEOFF SIMPSON

HALSGROVE

First published in Great Britain in 2011

British Library Cataloguing-in-Publication Data
A CIP record for this title is available from the British Library

ISBN 978 0 85704 114 2

HALSGROVE
Halsgrove House,
Ryelands Business Park,
Bagley Road, Wellington, Somerset TA21 9PZ
Tel: 01823 653777   Fax: 01823 216796
email: sales@halsgrove.com

Part of the Halsgrove group of companies
Information on all Halsgrove titles is available at: www.halsgrove.com

Printed and bound in the UK by the MPG Books Group

CONTENTS

ACKNOWLEDGEMENTS

Historians, authors and researchers who have shared their knowledge with me include:-

Colonel Pierre-Alain Antoine; Frank Armstrong; Gerry Burke; Alan Cooper; Sebastian Cox; Philip Curtis; Air Commodore Alex Dickson, OBE QVRM AE; Fred Dunster; Tony Edwards; Squadron Leader Beryl Escott; Edgar Evans; Fik Geuens; Michael Ginns, MBE; Group Captain Tom Gleave, CBE; Gary Godel; Geoffrey Goodman, CBE, DFC; John Grehan; Bob Hilton; CBE; Richard Hunting, Wing Commander C G Jefford, MBE; Peter Knottley; Michael Korda; Michael Long; Martin Mace; Patrick Mackreth; Edward McManus; Dr Tony Mansell; Geneviève Moulard; Michael Paul; Air Commodore Graham Pitchfork, MBE; Dr Sebastian Ritchie; Squadron Leader Tim Sindall; Group Captain Patrick Tootal, OBE, DL; John White; Kenneth G Wynne.

Richard Hunting has been an especial source of encouragement and help throughout the writing of this book.

I am also deeply grateful to Douglas Radcliffe, MBE, Secretary of the Bomber Command Association and to the many veterans of Bomber Command, aircrew and otherwise, who have talked to me about their experiences over many years.

A visit to the library of the Royal Air Force Club is always fruitful. The Guernsey Society and Sark Tourism gave particular help with the entry on Prisoners of War.

INTRODUCTION

When I first met Colin Ward, DFM he was in his early 80s. Colin was rather small, cheerful, friendly, hospitable, always well turned out and with the kind of manners often described as "impeccable" and sometimes now regarded as old fashioned.

He had done well in a long career, mostly in insurance and despite being a north Londoner, from Winchmore Hill, lived in a large, attractive and comfortable cottage in the rural part of the Jersey parish of St Saviour, with Margaret, the lady who would become his second wife.

It so happened that Colin had as friends members of the families of two Spitfire pilots killed in the Battle of Britain and, to further the research I was doing, had offered to introduce me to the brother in law of one of them.

Before I visited Colin for the first time at the cottage I knew that there was one thing about him that made him stand out in a crowd; that is if he was not wearing a hat. He had an enormous scar on his head.

That scar had been acquired, along with eventual membership of The Guinea Pig Club, in a gallant and horrifying episode in 1942 when Colin was a Wellington bomber pilot. Some of the story is told in The Guinea Pig Club entry in this book.

Colin died, aged 94, in 2008 and probably would not have approved of being picked out in this way.

I've done so because I feel that he illustrates so much about the 125,000 men of Bomber Command who flew into action in the Second World War. They volunteered on our behalf, they flew constantly into great danger, always facing the strong possibility of death and disfigurement in the most horrible of circumstances.

Many of those who survived went back into communities around the world and carried on with interrupted lives, seeking to keep the darker memories under control and, perhaps, also trying to ignore their depiction on occasions as the unacceptable manifestation of Britain's efforts in the Second World War.

That a man such as Colin Ward and the experience that he went through can be argued to be "typical" of Bomber Command aircrew between 1939 and 1945, surely makes the point that in this book and many others tribute is paid to a remarkable group of men.

Geoff Simpson
4 May 2011

AUTHOR'S NOTES

Where I have referred to someone's military rank during the Second World War I have normally used the rank in which that person was operating at the time irrespective of whether it was substantive or not.

Sir Arthur Harris is a special case, not least because of his considerable presence in any account of Bomber Command in the war. Seeking to avoid confusion I have erred on the side of referring to him, in his Bomber Command years, as "Air Chief Marshal Harris" and "Sir Arthur".

In fact he became a Knight Commander of the Order of the Bath on June 11 1942 and an acting Air Chief Marshal on March 18 1943. At the end of the war his substantive rank was Air Vice-Marshal. He became a Marshal of the Royal Air Force on January 1 1946. In 1953 he was made a Baronet.

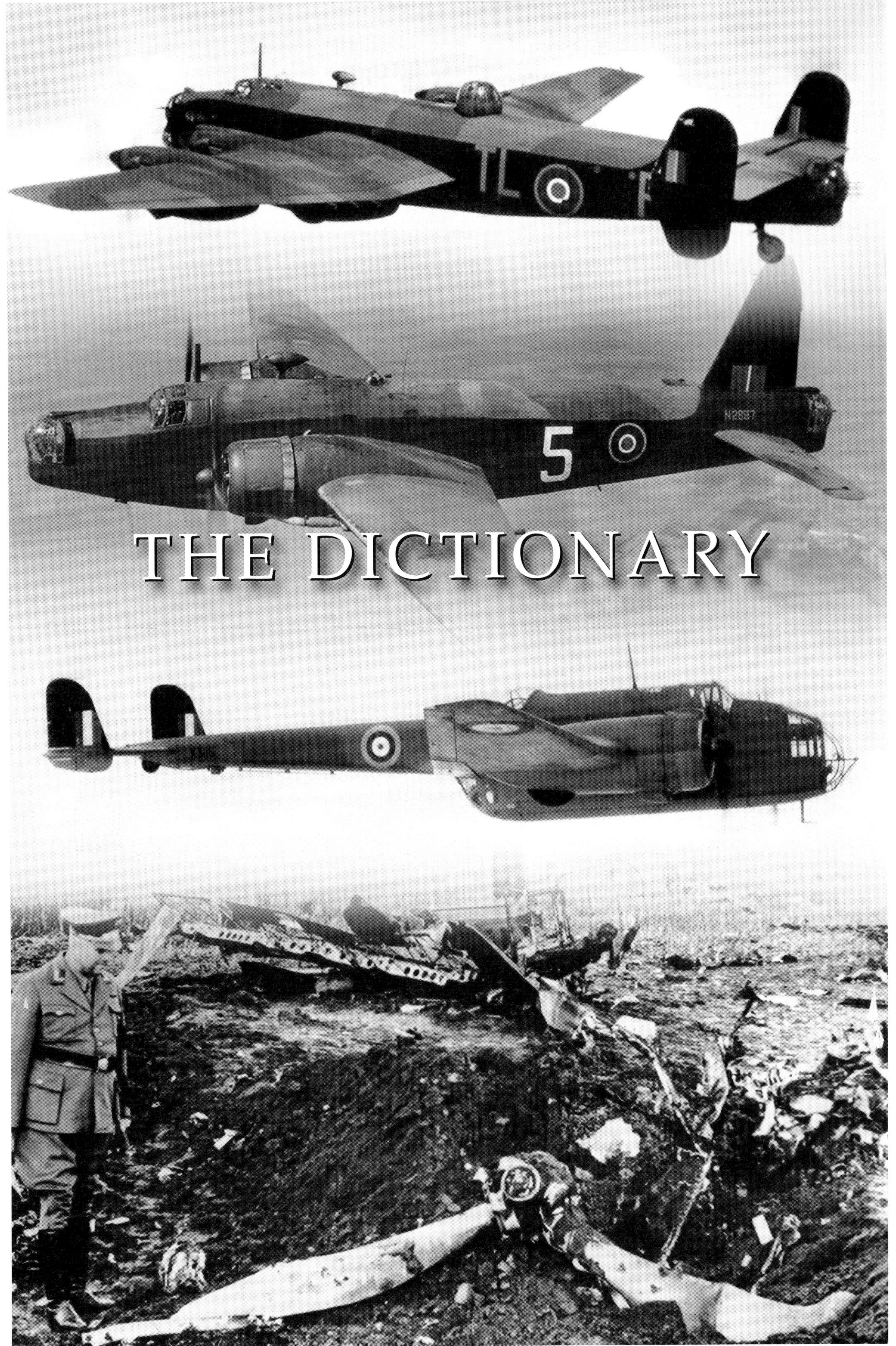

THE DICTIONARY

"There are no words with which I can do justice to the aircrew who fought under my command. There is no parallel in warfare to such courage and determination in the face of danger over so prolonged a period, of danger which at times was so great that scarcely one man in three could expect to survive his tour of operations." Marshal of the Royal Air Force Sir Arthur Harris writing in *Bomber Offensive*, 1947.

The two vertical aerials visible on the fuselage of this Lancaster were part of the Airborne Cigar equipment which jammed radio signals of German night fighter controllers.

Airborne Cigar (ABC) – One of the Radio Counter Measures (RCMs) designed to aid Bomber Command in overcoming German defences.

From October 1943 Lancasters of No 101 Squadron flew from Ludford Magna in the bomber stream with an eighth crew member known as the Special Duties Operator (SDO). Colloquially they were "Specials".

These men spoke fluent German and their job and that of their equipment was to jam the transmission of the German night fighter ground controllers. Each SDO used his knowledge of German to identify three frequencies on which the enemy controllers were transmitting and jammed them by broadcasting engine noise. In theory eight Lancasters operating in this way could blot out all transmissions.

The Germans developed the technology to find the engine noise transmissions and significant RAF casualties resulted.

An earlier version of ABC was ground-based but achieved limited success.

Aircrew Age – Some of the men who flew into action with Bomber Command were as young as 18 and many were in their 20s. On the other hand, especially amongst the Air Gunners, there were aircrew born in the reigns of King Edward Vll and Queen Victoria.

Chorley in *Bomber Command Losses, vol 1* suggests that a gunner in the crew of a Wellington lC of No 37 Squadron, flying from Feltwell, that crashed south of Dunkirk on the night of May 31/June 1 1940, may have been the oldest man to be lost on Bomber Command operations.

This was Pilot Officer Sir Arnold Wilson, born on July 18 1884 and therefore 55 at the time of his death. Sir Arnold had achieved the King's Medal and Sword of Honour at the Royal Military College, Sandhurst, had served in the 32nd Sikh Pioneers and the Indian Political Department and had been made DSO in 1916 after reconnoitring a position under Turkish fire. In 1933 he became MP for Hitchin, Hertfordshire as a National Conservative and in 1939 he volunteered for the RAF.

Another instance of someone who was considerably older than the average age was Flight Sergeant Robert George Gumbley. He was a Flight Engineer lost on the night of June 25/26 1942, when a Halifax ll of No 35 Squadron was hit by flak on an operation to Bremen. Two survivors became PoWs, but Gumbley, who was 42, is buried in Sage War Cemetery in northern Germany, along with the pilot, Flying Officer H G B Mays and other crew members, Pilot Officer S F Hazleton, Sergeant A J Selby and Sergeant R W Fisher.

Aiming Point – The key point in the target area as seen through the bomb aimer's bomb sight.

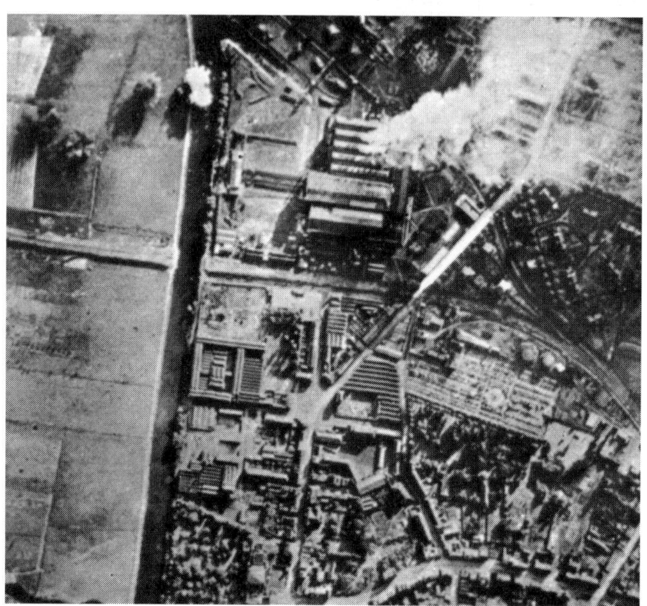

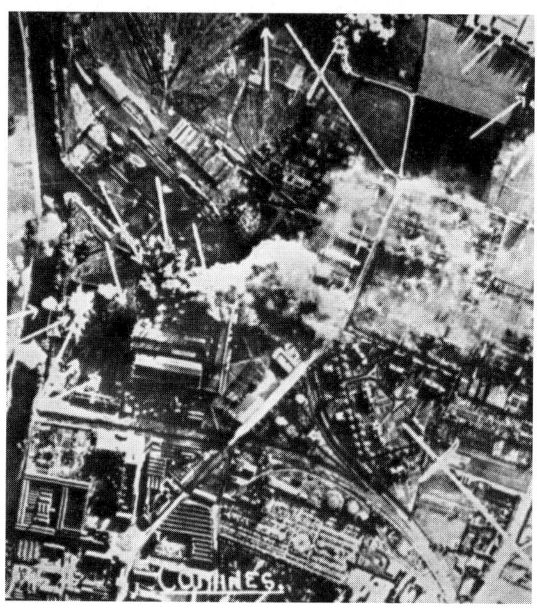

A power station at Comines in northern France before and after an attack.

Airfields – Many travellers on the eastern side of England today, from County Durham to Suffolk must pass through towns, villages and districts and see them as insignificant. To the wartime generation of airmen some of the names are lodged for a lifetime in their minds.

Croft, Middleton St George, Holme on Spalding Moor, Pocklington, Lindholme, Elsham Wolds, Binbrook, Swinderby, Hemswell, Scampton, Coningsby, Ludford Magna, Woodhall Spa, Horsham St Faith, Downham Market, Swanton Morley, Great Massingham, Mildenhall, Stradishall, Syerston, Woolfox Lodge, Bottesford, Newmarket and

At Oakington a No 7 Squadron Stirling comes into land.

Wyton. These are just a few of the names that resonate, for better or worse, with Bomber Command veterans.

Lodged too in those memories are the variations in facilities between the pre-war airfields, such as Binbrook and those constructed at speed during the course of the conflict of which Woodhall Spa was one example. Some had concrete runways and some were grass. Many airmen too recalled in post war days the journey eastwards by wartime train and the first view of a new home, perhaps through driving rain and across the Lincolnshire fields of root crops.

"It was a terrible place, cold, bleak, isolated. We faced a two mile walk to our huts, which were as bad as you would find anywhere in the RAF. They were draughty, ran with condensation and we had so little fuel for the single stove that some of the Aussies on the squadron took to stealing other people's doors to burn. By the time I left there was hardly a lavatory door left." Eric Brown a Flight Engineer on No 106 Squadron, recalling Metheringham and quoted by Patrick Otter in *Lincolnshire Airfields of the Second World War*.

To be fair, it also needs to be said that there were those who enjoyed their service and camp life, including the frequent visits to local pubs that, for many, were a key means of entertainment in rural locations.

"Let us now take a glance at the station itself. It is in most cases of recent construction and the layout follows up-to-date principles. The buildings, camouflaged so as to cause them to blend as far as possible with the colours and contours of the surrounding country, are constructed in blocks with considerable space between them and over a wide area.

"A network of roads connects them with station headquarters where the operations room is situated, with the officers' and sergeants' messes, with the quarters of the men, with those of the WAAF, with the hospital and decontamination centre, with the bomb dump, with the hangars and with the airfield itself, which is surrounded by a perimeter track. For obvious reasons aircraft no longer live in hangars. They are dispersed round the field in such a way as to minimise any effects which may be caused by bombing. They remain and are serviced in the open air, only being taken to the hangars for some major repair."

From *Bomber Command*, Air Ministry official publication 1941.

From March 1943 a "base" system was set up, whereby groups of airfields became a headquarters with perhaps two satellites and some centralised facilities.

Air Gunner – "These men were sat in a very cramped position for seven to eight hours with an oxygen supply.

Peter Turley, DFM in the rear turret of the Battle of Britain Memorial Flight Lancaster, Phantom of the Ruhr. Sadly Peter is now blind.

Photograph Gary Godel.

"They were often exposed to the outside elements because they sometimes removed the perspex in front of them to get a clearer view. It'd be so cold that icicles would drop off their oxygen masks.

"It was a tough job – and it wasn't just about going on the attack.

"They played an important defensive role by passing the knowledge of what was around them to the pilot who could then manoeuvre the aircraft out of the way.

"They also had to have a certain intelligence to do the job. Maths was important to know when to open fire at certain distances and they had to know about the machine guns they were using." Douglas Radcliffe, Secretary of the Bomber Command Association, explaining the role of the rear gunner to a local newspaper.

A number of Royal Artillery officers flew as air gunners so that they could experience anti-aircraft fire from the "wrong end".

Air Transport Auxiliary – Organisation established in 1939 following a proposal by Gerard d'Erlanger, a director of the then British Airways – his original concept involved a pool of civilian pilots carrying out such duties as the ferrying of mail, medical and other light supplies and ambulance work. However, aircraft delivery soon became a major task.

Many ATA pilots were men considered unsuitable for operational flying, through age or other cause. They took to referring to themselves as "Ancient and Tattered Airmen".

A women's section, led by Pauline Gower, was established in 1940. Women flew all types of aircraft except amphibians off water. They also acted as flight engineers on four-engined aircraft such as the Lancaster. Well known female pilots in the ATA included Amy Johnson, Lettice Curtis (credited with flying 222 Halifaxs and 109 Stirlings) and Diana Barnato.

The ATA does its stuff.

ATA personnel delivered Fairey Battles to France in May 1940, aircraft to Fighter Command airfields during the Battle of Britain and flew into Europe again after D-Day.

Before its disbandment at the end of the war the ATA had delivered 309,011 aircraft and suffered 174 aircrew deaths.

Aldis Lamp – A signalling lamp invented by Arthur Aldis which was produced in various sizes. Such lamps were used for signalling from aircraft, often by means of Morse Code.

The tale is told of the normally excellent navigator who slipped up one night on the return from Europe and brought his Wellington in over the docks at Harwich. Every gun in the place opened up and various attempts to achieve recognition failed.

Eventually the Wireless Operator caused all the firing to cease. Using a mixture of indelicate language and a service name for sailors he signalled "F——— Jacks" with his Aldis Lamp. The Navy apparently took the view that no German could possibly think of that.

Area Bombing – In the early years of the war RAF bombing was criticised for lack of accuracy and effectiveness.

Aircraft had inadequate navigation aids and generally flew at night to minimise losses to enemy fighters and anti-aircraft fire.

From 1942 Bomber Command was ordered by the Air Ministry, at the instigation of the War Cabinet, to carry out area bombing of German cities, which required less accuracy. In this way cities, rather than individual specified industrial and military targets within the cities, were subjected to raids. The British Government justified the policy by declaring that cities were the basis of the German war effort and economy and that bombing cities would wear down the morale of the German people.

Despite wartime restrictions on communication the policy suffered severe and public criticism.

A leading and high profile opponent of area bombing was Bishop George Bell, former Dean of Canterbury and from 1929 Bishop of Chichester. Bell had campaigned against the Nazi regime from its earliest days. During the war he sought to encourage those plotting to remove Hitler and he also attacked Britain's air policy. This was opposition at a very high level. Bell was close to becoming Archbishop of Canterbury when Archbishop Temple died in 1944.

Other prominent opponents of area bombing were the Labour MPs Richard Stokes and Dr Alfred Salter.

Armstrong Whitworth Whitley – A medium bomber, the Whitley first flew in March 1936. A year later operational examples of the Whitley 1 began to arrive at Dishforth for No 10 Squadron. The name derived from the Coventry district of Whitley, the location of an Armstrong Whitworth plant.

In its early form the aircraft was fitted with two Armstrong Siddeley Tiger engines, many later examples would have power provided by Rolls Royce Merlins. The bomb load was up to 7,000lb and there were nose and tail turrets for defence, with a retractable ventral turret in some aircraft.

The Whitley was produced in large numbers during the early war years.

A 2000lb bomb lies waiting for the armourers to load it aboard a Whitley Mk V in 1941.

From the first day of the war and until the advent of the "heavies", the Whitley was a key element of Bomber Command. The Whitley's last operational contribution to the bomber offensive was the 1,000 aircraft attack on Cologne on May 30/31 1942 when OTU aircraft and crews were added to the attack.

Whitleys served in Coastal Command patrolling the Western Approaches. They were also used to train glider tug pilots and paratroops, in the latter role operating from Ringway, Manchester. Whitleys also dropped agents and supplied

resistance groups in occupied countries and – unarmed and operated by BOAC – flew supplies from Gibraltar to Malta.

Avro Lancaster – The aircraft that has come to symbolise the Bomber Command effort in The Second World War, despite the successes achieved by other types.

The spearhead of the Bomber Offensive – Avro Lancasters in flight.

In 1940 the Avro design team, led by Chief Designer Roy Chadwick, was working on a four-engined version of the Avro Manchester which would utilise Rolls Royce Merlin engines. With the Merlin much in demand at the time to power Hurricane and Spitfire fighters the Air Ministry was not initially encouraging, however a request to go ahead with the project was made in the middle of the year, with the proviso that as many Manchester components as possible should be used.

The first flight of a prototype took place on January 9 1941. The design was considered a success, as demonstrated in

A Lancaster crew of No 75 (New Zealand) Squadron about to take off for Wesel, March 1945 – their last op and they came home.
Courtesy Neville Selwood.

many test flights in a short period, however a new tail section was designed before the first production model flew on May 13 1941. The next month Avro received a contract to produce 454 Lancaster Mk 1s, with four Merlin XX engines and, in addition, there was a requirement to turn out two prototype Lancaster Mk lls with Bristol Hercules Vl engines.

On December 24 1941 No 44 Squadron, which was based at Waddington, Lincolnshire became the first squadron in Bomber Command to receive Lancasters. The earliest Lancaster participation in an operation occurred on March 3 1942 when four of the type from No 44 Squadron laid mines in the Heligoland Bight between the mouth of the River Elbe and the Heligoland Islands.

The normal bomb load of the Lancaster was up to 14,000lb, though much heavier single bombs were carried in aircraft with modified bomb bays. Nose and dorsal turrets were provided, with two 0.303in Browning machine guns, while the rear turret had four Brownings. Maximum speed was of the order of 275 mph, with a cruising speed of 200 mph. The service ceiling was 22,000 ft and the range just over 2,500 miles.

With the emphasis placed on the importance of four-engined bombers from 1942 Rolls Royce envisaged difficulties in meeting the demand for Merlin engines, hence the use of the Bristol Hercules in the Mk ll Lancaster and the production of Merlins by Packard in the United States. Lancasters powered by the American-built engines were known as Mk llls.

Over 7000 Lancasters were built and 57 Bomber Command squadrons were equipped with them during the Second World War.

Post-war uses of the Lancaster included in-flight re-fuelling (in which role it participated in the Berlin Air Lift) and as a freighter by British South American Airways.

Opposite page: Lancaster Mk 1s of No 207 Squadron, June 1942.

EM C
EM A
EM F

In 1943 a Lancaster IV was planned, but this went on to become the Type 694 Lincoln which, as a result of some delays and the Japanese surrender, did not see operational service in the Second World War. The type did serve in Kenya and Malaya and the last Lincoln left RAF service in 1963.

Today the Lancaster lives on most prominently in the shape of the aircraft operated by the Battle of Britain Memorial Flight.

Avro Manchester – A medium bomber with two Rolls Royce Vulture engines, the Manchester first flew in July 1939. The first squadron to receive the type was No 207 in late 1940.

Problems with both the engines and the airframe ensured that the Manchester has gone down in history as a failure. It is reckoned that of the 202 built around a quarter were written off in crashes. However, the other side of the coin is that the far more successful Lancaster, with four engines, was developed from the Manchester.

A pilot who experienced the problems of the Manchester was Sergeant Les Syrett, who flew 18 operations on them with No 207 Squadron. His first trip was to Brest in February 1941, as second pilot, but when the pilot was wounded Syrett took over the controls, completed the bombing run and brought the aircraft back. He received an immediate DFM.

The Avro Manchester – an ill fated design which led to the Lancaster.

On June 21 1941 Sergeant Syrett took off from Waddington on an air test. Almost immediately both engines cut out and the Manchester plunged into a field. Syrett survived, despite injuries that included a broken neck and back and became a member of The Guinea Pig Club. With him in the aircraft were Squadron Leader C J F Kydd who was killed and Flight Sergeant J W Arnott, who died of his injuries a month later.

Barges, Battle of – Name given to the attacks by Bomber Command, in which Coastal Command and the Fleet Air Arm also participated, on the river barges being assembled across the Channel, as part of the German preparations for invasion. From the beginning of July 1940 missions were flown, with heavy losses, against barge concentrations in such locations as Ostend, Le Havre, Boulogne, Dunkirk, Antwerp and the Dortmund-Ems canal.

"The Station Commander gathered all officers together one morning in August or September 1940 and told us that it appeared invasion was imminent and that we should be prepared for it. I remember the silence that followed. We left the room and I don't think anyone spoke, but we were all the more determined to make certain that we did everything possible to deter the Germans from launching their invasion.

"At the time we were bombing the invasion barges in the Channel ports, undertaking operations almost every other night. I remember one operation in particular against the invasion barges. We had part moonlight, which was very helpful because navigation in those days depended entirely on visual identification. We flew to the north of our target so that we could get a better outline of the coast. We followed the coast down towards our target, getting down to about 4,000 feet so that we could get a better view of what was below, and to increase the accuracy of the bombing. At that height light anti-aircraft fire was pretty heavy and fairly accurate so we didn't hang around after dropping our bombs. This was done repeatedly over a period of time until the invasion was called off."

Air Commodore Wilf Burnett quoted on the Bomber Command Association website.

"Dunkirk, September 14 (1940) – Barges

"We were airborne at base (Hemswell) at 19.55 hrs and set course from Lincoln at 20.02 hrs. At 20.51 hrs we crossed the English coast on our outward journey and arrived in the target area at 21.30 hrs. The searchlights and anti-aircraft fire was intense, but we were able to recognise the target area. We made three attempts to drop our bombs but the fire was so intense that we were obliged to make a fourth run-in. This was done with the engine throttled back. The bombs were dropped in the target area but owing to the avoiding action taken by the pilot it was impossible to see the bursts. The journey home was uneventful and we landed at base at 23.20 hrs."

Sergeant Bob Pearman, who in 1940/41 flew a tour as a Hampden pilot with No 144 Squadron, describes an early sortie, in which he participated as a second pilot, in the book *Burford Boy*.

"The barges collecting against us in the invasion ports were very different {to the traditional image of a British canal barge}. German, Dutch, Belgian and French barges are of all sizes up to 3,000 tons carrying capacity, although the largest are few in number and limited to special trades. The most common type can carry between 300 and 400 tons and if self-propelled has a speed of about eight knots.

"The Germans decided to use barges for two main reasons. In the first place they were ready to hand ———-. In the second place a barge is peculiarly suitable for the transport of vehicles which have to be landed in a hurry, perhaps in the face of hostile fire. To land a tank or an armoured car or a lorry on to a beach from an ordinary ship is extremely difficult."

From the 1941 Air Ministry publication, *Bomber Command.* It estimated that in September 1940 the enemy had at least 3,000 self propelled barges available for use, with many more thousands to be towed by tugs.

Battle of Britain – Following the fall of France in June 1940, the Germans sought to establish air dominance over southern England and the English Channel, thus opening up the possibility of invasion.

Sergeant Bert Black, a bomber pilot who volunteered for Fighter Command and was fatally wounded in action in the Battle of Britain. Courtesy Battle of Britain Memorial Trust.

Bomber Command played a crucial part in ensuring that invasion never became feasible, attacking barge concentrations in Channel ports (see entry for Battle of the Barges) and many other targets.

In his "Never in the Field of Human Conflict" speech to the House of Commons on August 20 1940, Winston Churchill, as Prime Minister, declared:-

"The gratitude of every home in our Island, in our Empire, and indeed throughout the world, except in the abodes of the guilty, goes out to the British airmen who, undaunted by odds, unwearied in their constant challenge and mortal danger, are turning the tide of the World War by their prowess and by their devotion. Never in the field of human conflict was so much owed by so many to so few. All hearts go out to the fighter pilots, whose brilliant actions we see with our own eyes day after day; but we must never forget that all the time, night after night, month after month, our bomber squadrons travel far into Germany, find their targets in the darkness by the highest navigational skill, aim their attacks, often under the heaviest fire, often with serious loss, with deliberate careful discrimination, and inflict shattering blows upon the whole of the technical and war-making structure of the Nazi power. On no part of the Royal Air Force does the weight of the war fall more heavily than on the daylight bombers, who will play an invaluable part in the case of invasion and whose unflinching zeal it has been necessary in the meanwhile on numerous occasions to restrain.

"We are able to verify the results of bombing military targets in Germany, not only by reports which reach us through many sources, but also, of course, by photography. I have no hesitation in saying that this process of bombing the military industries and communications of Germany and the air bases and storage depots from which we are attacked, which process will continue upon an ever-increasing scale until the end of the war, and may in another year attain dimensions hitherto undreamed of, affords one at least of the most certain, if not the shortest, of all the roads to victory. Even if the Nazi legions stood triumphant on the Black Sea, or indeed upon the Caspian, even if Hitler was at the gates of India, it would profit him nothing if at the same time the entire economic and scientific apparatus of German war power lay shattered and pulverized at home."

Ever since this speech was delivered, its precise meaning has been debated. The term "The Few" has become attached to the airmen of RAF Fighter Command and Churchill confirmed this interpretation when he penned The Second World War, Volume ll, *Their Finest Hour*. Here he wrote:-

"At the summit (of endeavour in the Battle of Britain) the stamina and valour of our fighter pilots remained unconquerable and supreme. Thus Britain was saved. Well might I say in the House of Commons, 'Never in the field of human conflict was so much owed by so many to so few.'"

Pressure to list those who had taken part in the Battle of Britain and to give them an emblem to wear had begun very early.

In July 1942 Captain Bruce Ingram (later Sir Bruce), proprietor of the Illustrated London News, wrote to the Secretary of State for Air, comparing the importance of the Battle in British history with the defeat of the Armada and the Battle of Trafalgar. He proposed that a permanent record of those who had played "an active part" should be created. He offered to arrange for the creation of a scroll with the names inscribed in gold leaf. This would be presented to Westminster Abbey or another institution.

While Sir Archibald Sinclair Bt, the Secretary of State, was supportive, the difficulties of undertaking the research in wartime were immediately put forward, as was the problem of recognising the contribution made by all RAF Commands.

On August 19 1942 the Air Council concluded that a roll of honour should be prepared of Fighter Command personnel killed in the Battle. This was not what Ingram wanted and he wrote that the scroll should contain, "the names of the pilots of the fighter planes that went into the air to defend Britain, as it is obvious that one who came through the ordeal was just as great a hero as one who was killed in the action."

The official plan, however, proceeded and a scroll was prepared by the calligrapher, Daisy Alcock, which eventually included the names of both fighter and bomber aircrew lost during the Battle. This was presented to Westminster Abbey in 1947 at the same time as the Abbey's RAF chapel and Battle of Britain window were unveiled by the King. Relatives of Fighter and Bomber aircrew lost in the Battle period were invited to attend.

By this point the fundamental definition of the Battle of Britain had been established along with entitlement to the immediate award of the 1939-45 Star, with Battle of Britain Clasp, the only Clasp to be awarded with that Star.

On May 24 1945 Air Ministry Order, A532/1945 was issued and stated that:-

"A clasp to the 1939-45 Star has been instituted for air crew of fighter aircraft engaged in the Battle of Britain between the 1st July and the 31st October, 1940, and the award of this is to be denoted by a gilt rose Emblem when the ribbon alone is worn."

Air Ministry Order A741/1945 July 23 1945 listed qualifying squadrons (there were subsequent modifications) and announced that the first qualifying date was changed to July 10 1940. This AMO stressed that, "COs are not to admit claims for this highly-prized emblem which are open to any possible doubt. The clasp is not available for personnel who flew in aircraft other than fighters, notwithstanding that they may have been engaged with the enemy in the air during the qualifying period."

So, for better or worse, eligibility for the Battle of Britain Clasp was firmly established and all non-aircrew were excluded, as well as those who had flown in Bomber and Coastal Commands. Some Fleet Air Arm personnel qualified for the award, both those who had been attached to Fighter Command squadrons during the Battle and members of two FAA squadrons included in the final list of units as they had been under the control of Fighter Command.

As Fighter Command losses in the Battle mounted Bomber Command and Army Co-operation pilots were asked to volunteer to fly fighters. Among the bomber pilots who answered this call were Sergeant Bert Black, Flying Officer Michael Homer and Flight Lieutenant Tony O'Neill. Black had flown Fairey Battles in France with No 226 Squadron while Homer had earned a DFC with No 106 Squadron (Hampdens) on April 6 1940 during an operation against enemy shipping in the harbour at Kristiansand, Norway. O'Neill, also a holder of the DFC, had dropped leaflets over Germany on September 3/4 1939, flying a Whitley of No 58 Squadron, finishing off the night in a French cabbage field.

Black was shot down, flying a Hurricane of No 46 Squadron, on October 29 1940 and died of his wounds 11 days later. Homer was killed in action with another Hurricane squadron, No 242, on September 28 1940, while O'Neill survived his service as a Hurricane pilot with Nos 601 and 238 Squadrons and was a retired Group Captain when he died in 2008.

Some pilots and other aircrew who had flown in fighters and qualified for the Clasp later served in Bomber Command. Examples of Bomber Command pilots who had earlier gained entitlement to the Battle of Britain Clasp, were Squadron Leader Tony Iveson and Flight Lieutenant Edward Cranwell (both Spitfire pilots before transferring to bombers) and Squadron Leader Jerrard Latimer who, as Jerrard

Jefferies, had been a Hurricane pilot in 1940. He was lost in 1943, flying as a second pilot in a Lancaster of No 106 Squadron.

Edward Cranwell, despite his name, had been a Sergeant pilot in the Battle of Britain. Much later Tony Iveson would be a long-serving Chairman of the Bomber Command Association.

Berchtesgaden – On April 25 1945 359 Lancasters and 16 Mosquitos attacked Hitler's "Eagle's Nest" home and the accompanying SS barracks in the Bavarian Alps above the town of Berchtesgaden. One objective was to obviate the possibility of Hitler using the location to set up an "Alpine Redoubt". Much damage was done.

Berlin – The German capital and therefore a major propaganda prize, not least after the promises made by the German leadership that the RAF would not be able to operate over Berlin. That claim was disproved in 1940.

Later Air Chief Marshal Harris put forward the proposition that to achieve destruction in Berlin on the scale of what had been achieved in Hamburg could lead to German capitulation.

While attacks on Berlin took place on many occasions, the "Battle of Berlin" was the 16 attacks mounted through the winter of 1943/44.

The "Battle" opened on the night of November 18/19 1943, with 440 Lancasters and four Mosquitos tasked to go to Berlin, with a considerable force of Lancasters, Stirlings and Halifaxs mounting a diversionary attack on Mannheim. Poor weather, which had not been predicted, reduced the effectiveness of both raids, though some significant damage was caused. British casualties were heavier on the Mannheim attack than they were amongst those who flew to Berlin.

By the time the onslaught on Berlin ended in March 1944 it was clear that nothing like the impact predicted had been achieved, despite the loss to Bomber Command of around 500 aircraft.

Big City – Name applied by Bomber Command personnel to the German capital, Berlin.

Boeing B-17 Flying Fortress – The B-17 was created following a US Army specification of 1934 calling for a long-range, high-altitude daylight bomber. Though it went on to become one of the most famous bombers of all time, the B-17's mainstream career in RAF Bomber Command, with No 90 Squadron, was brief, there was a range of problems and the design was already looking dated compared with other four-engined bombers that were becoming available.

Some B-17s were operated by No 223 Squadron for electronic jamming and intelligence operations.

This B-17C was one of the first of the type to fly with the RAF.

Bomb Aimer (or Air Bomber) – The man who was effectively in charge of the aircraft over the target, calling course corrections to the pilot, ordering the opening of the bomb doors and releasing the bombs. Determined and competent Bomb Aimers might indicate that it was necessary to "go round again", but this was not the way to popularity with the rest of the crew.

Bombs fall during a raid on occupied France. Photographs played a key role in determining the success of an attack and the performance of individual crews.

On the Dams raid in May 1943 some bomb aimers, naturally in the circumstances, sought to get as close to perfection as possible. For example, Sergeant G L Johnson in Flight Lieutenant McCarthy's Lancaster did not release his Upkeep mine until the aircraft's 10th run over the Sorpe Dam. At this point he could detect some unrest amongst the rest of the crew. Johnson's perseverance was rewarded with a DFM.

Sometimes comrades could be more sympathetic:-

"In 1941 it was not uncommon to go round again if you couldn't see the target. At Brest going for the *Scharnhorst* and *Gneisenau*, we went round again twice.

"In 1944 in daylight on a flying bomb launch site we went round again twice and had two engines knocked out for our pains.

"On all occasions none blamed the Bomb Aimer for the cloud got in the way at the wrong moment."

Lord Sandhurst speaking in 2002. He was The Hon "Sandy" Mansfield in his days as a Bomb Aimer.

Bomber Barons – A term used in the media and elsewhere to denote senior and long serving bomber airmen.

Safely home: An exhausted crew return from a mission over Germany.

Bomber Command – Five RAF Commands were created at the time of the RAF expansion plan of 1935, when Air Defence of Great Britain, created in 1925 became defunct. The new Commands were Bomber, Fighter, Coastal, Training and Maintenance. Bomber Command officially came into existence on July 14 1936 and merged with Fighter Command to form Strike Command on April 30 1968.

Bomber Command Association – Organisation formed in 1985 to maintain comradeship and perpetuate the Command's history. Membership is available to all "who served in Bomber Command, the V-Force, Strike Command or in associated Allied Air Forces, regardless of rank or trade." Others may become associate members. The headquarters are at the RAF Museum, Hendon.

The Association's objectives are, "To promote the efficiency of the Royal Air Force and preserve its traditions by maintaining contact between past and present members of Bomber Command and Strike Command, fostering esprit-de-corps and comradeship.

"To support the charitable work of the Bomber Command Hall (of the RAF Museum) and other projects which educate and inform the general public in the work and history of Bomber Command and the V-Force."

Bomber Command Museum – The idea of a Bomber Command Museum had been much discussed, with attention focussed on whether it should be a discrete operation or based at the RAF Museum at Hendon. Some concern was expressed that the latter might result in it being overshadowed by the Battle of Britain Museum already on the Hendon site.

That concern was shared by Sir Arthur Harris, but he favoured Hendon as the location nonetheless. He immersed himself in the detail of the project and took a leading role in fund raising.

The Bomber Command Museum at Hendon was opened on April 12 1963 by Her Majesty Queen Elizabeth the Queen Mother. Later it became known as the Bomber Command Hall and is now the Bomber Hall.

In early 2011 the collection of aircraft included a Vickers Wellington X, an Avro Lancaster 1, a Handley Page Halifax ll and a Boeing B 17G Fortress. Aircraft from later eras included a Blackburn Buccaneer S2B and a Panavia Tornado GR1A.

"The spectacular success of the Battle of Britain is common knowledge, but the efforts of many men, particularly in Bomber Command, have in the main been forgotten. The Bomber Command Museum, Hendon presents a special opportunity for the nation to remember what was achieved in quest of peace." From the introduction to an undated, but early, guidebook to the Museum.

Bomber Stream – Tactic employed from 1942 intended to overwhelm the German night fighters and their electronic support. Rather than individual navigators plotting their way to the target, aircraft were allotted positions in the stream.

Bottomley, Air Chief Marshal Sir Norman Howard (1891-1970) – Born in the "Heavy Woollen" district of the West Riding of Yorkshire, the son of a journeyman cotton spinner, Bottomley served in France as an officer in the East Yorkshire Regiment. He was seconded to the Royal Flying Corps, flew operationally and was awarded the AFC.

With a permanent commission as a Flight Lieutenant, Bottomley served on the RAF staff in Cairo. He became a student at the RAF Staff College, Andover and undertook a tour of duty in the Directorate of Operations and Intelligence at the Air Ministry. Bottomley commanded No 4 Squadron, in an army co-operation role, studied at the Imperial Defence College and instructed at the RAF Staff College. From 1934 to 1938 he was in India, becoming a substantive Group Captain in 1935. He played a leading role in suppressing unrest in Waziristan and received the DSO.

Bottomley returned to the UK and went to Bomber Command as SASO to Air Chief Marshal Ludlow-Hewitt. From July 1 1940 Bottomley was a substantive Air Vice-Marshal and that November he took command of No 5 Group. In May 1941 he was appointed Deputy Chief of the Air Staff. For a time the post was abolished and his title was

Assistant Chief of the Air Staff (Operations), he reverted to the title of DCAS when that post was reinstated. He was made KCB in 1943.

Bottomley worked closely with Air Chief Marshal Harris on a day to day basis and cordial exchanges were possible though the relationship could be as difficult as that of some other Air Ministry figures with Harris. Bottomley was clearly an outstanding administrator, though Wilfrid Freeman (Vice Chief of the Air Staff 1940-42) considered that he lacked stamina and capacity for work.

On September 15 1945 Sir Norman Bottomley, now an Air Marshal, succeeded Harris as AO C-in-C, Bomber Command. This appointment lasted until January 1947 when he became Inspector-General of the RAF, promotion to Air Chief Marshal coming two months later. He retired from the RAF in 1948.

Eight years followed in which Sir Norman made a major mark at the BBC as Director of Administration. He was acting Director-General in 1956/57.

Bristol Blenheim – The Blenheim emerged from a private venture – a desire by Lord Rothermere of the Daily Mail to have a fast and comfortable aircraft for his own use. A military version was developed and first flew in 1936.

When the Blenheim entered service in 1937 with No 114 Squadron in No 2 Group, it was seen as a most advanced aircraft. The first year of the war indicated how far it had slipped from that eminent position. Nonetheless, it was a Blenheim of No 139 Squadron that made the first wartime reconnaissance over Germany on September 3 1939 and the type flew in considerable numbers with Bomber Command in the early part of the conflict. Blenheims also equipped Fighter, Coastal and Army Co-operation Command squadrons, as well as serving in the Middle East and Far East.

RT

The Bristol Blenheim entered service with the RAF in 1937. This example was on the strength of a Fighter Command Operational Training Unit.

The Blenheim IV had two Bristol Mercury engines, a maximum speed of 266 mph, a ceiling of over 27,000 ft and a range of 1,460 miles. It had five 0.303 machine guns and could carry over 1,000lb of bombs.

Despite the losses suffered by the Blenheim squadrons, it was possible for aircraft to have considerable operational careers. Blenheim IV L9240 survived service with the AASF and more than 50 sorties in total before it was lost with No 18 Squadron on July 30 1941, flying from Horsham St Faith to attack the Kiel Canal. The crew of Sergeant H D Cue, Sergeant J M Jarrell, RCAF and Sergeant P C Brewer all became PoWs.

Bufton, Air Vice-Marshal Sydney Osborne (1908-1993) – Bufton was born in Wales and became an engineering student at Vickers before, in 1927, being accepted for RAF pilot training and travelling to Egypt for his course. Once qualified he flew Hawker Horsley bombers. He later instructed and took a course in aeronautical engineering.

"Buf" Bufton served in Iraq and at the Air Ministry, contributing to the pre-war expansion of the RAF. After the Staff College at Andover he was a staff officer in France in the early months of the war, returning to Britain in mid-June 1940.

Opposite page, top: A Bristol Blenheim is prepared for action.

Opposite page, bottom: A dramatic shot of Blenheims attacking a power station near Cologne.

Flying Whitley bombers was Bufton's next step and he took command of No 10 Squadron, participating in 19 operations and being awarded the DFC. On the night of October 27/28 1940 he suffered the loss of his youngest brother, Pilot Officer John Bufton, the skipper of a Hampden of No 49 Squadron shot down off Skegness, by an intruder, with no survivors.

Sydney Bufton commanded No 76 Squadron with Halifaxs and, as a Group Captain, was Officer Commanding Pocklington. On November 1 1941 he became Deputy Director, Bombing Operations at the Air Ministry, holding the post of Director from March 1943 to June 1945.

During his time in these Air Ministry positions Bufton found himself, along with some of his colleagues, at frequent odds with Arthur Harris. As somebody who had recently flown bomber operations, Bufton seemed to feel that Harris was out of touch with operational reality, as well as being an unapproachable figure. Harris did not appreciate outsiders, often considerably junior in rank, advising him on the conduct of his command.

The biggest clash occurred over what became the Pathfinder Force. Bufton was a campaigner for the idea and perhaps unscrupulous in attempts to out-manoeuvre Harris on the issue. Harris claimed not to dislike Bufton, but to dislike his methods.

In the post-war RAF appointments held by Bufton included Director of Weapons, Air Ministry, Air Officer Administration, Bomber Command, Air Officer Commanding British Forces, Aden and Assistant Chief of the Air Staff, Intelligence. He retired as an Air Vice-Marshal in 1961 and founded Radionic Products, which, eight years later, he sold to Philips.

Shortly after Sydney Bufton's death his widow, Mrs Susan Bufton, presented papers relating in particular to his wartime service to the Churchill Archive Centre at Churchill College, Cambridge.

Butt Report – A report on the effectiveness of Bomber Command operations prepared at the instigation of Lord Cherwell, by David M Bensusan-Butt, a young economist and civil servant working for the War Cabinet. The report was completed in August 1941 and caused much consternation at the Air Ministry and as high as the Prime Minister, with its demonstration of the inability of the RAF bomber force at that time to find and hit targets in anything approaching sufficient numbers.

A crew that has just returned from a raid discusses the outcome with intelligence officers.

Butt studied the impact on 28 German targets attacked in June and July 1941, using 633 aerial photographs taken in the aftermath of attacks. He concluded that only one in three aircraft dropped their bombs within five miles of the target. In the case of targets in the Ruhr the figure was much worse. Indeed, Butt's figures generally can be presented in an even worse light, because he excluded from his calculation aircraft that failed to reach the target area through accident, enemy action, weather, navigational failures and other causes.

At Bomber Command Sir Richard Peirse was not impressed with the findings, but the Butt Report can now be seen as a key contributor to the eventual departure of Peirse, the appointment of Harris to the Command and the prosecution of the policy of area bombing.

Campaign Awards – There was no specific award for the aircrew or groundcrew of Bomber Command, a fact that has rankled with many over the years.

Awards that could be earned included:-

The 1939-45 Star for aircrew who carried out operations against the enemy and completed two months of service on an operational unit. Non-flying personnel needed to achieve six months of service in the area of an overseas operational command. In both cases those who did not achieve the minimum period through death, wounds and some other causes still qualified for the award. Those separately awarded an honour, decoration, mention in despatches or King's Commendation qualified, even if they did not achieve the specified length of service.

The Aircrew Europe Star which was awarded to those who had qualified for the 1939-45 Star and had flown from the UK over Europe between September 3 1939 and June 5 1944. Two

(Left) The 1939-45 Star was awarded to British Commonwealth forces. Air Force personnel had to participate in operations against the enemy providing that two months' service had been completed in an operational unit. Non-aircrew personnel had to complete six months' service in an area of (overseas) operational command.

(Right) The Aircrew Europe Star was awarded for operational flying from United Kingdom bases over Europe between September 3 1939 to the June 4 1944. The period of qualification was two months.

months of service as aircrew was required, apart from those killed, wounded, etc.

The France and Germany Star, which was granted for service in France, Belgium, The Netherlands or Germany or operational service flying over Europe (outside the remit of the Italy Star) between June 6 1944 ("D Day") and May 8 1945.

Casualties – More than 55,000 aircrew lost their lives while serving with Bomber Command in the Second World War, around 44 per cent of the total of aircrew who served in the Command. Almost 9,000 operational aircraft were lost.

Flying through flak bursts – a Stirling in action.

Two letters typical of those received by next of kin, in this case a widow.

From the Air Ministry (Casualty Branch)

Dear Madam

I am commanded by the Air Council to state that in view of the lapse of time and the absence of any further news regarding your husband (rank and name), since the date on which he was reported missing, they must regretfully conclude that he has lost his life, and his death has now been presumed, for official purposes, to have occurred on (date).

The Council desire me to express again their sympathy with you in the anxiety which you have suffered, and in your bereavement.

I am, Madam, Your obedient Servant

From The Central Chancery of The Orders of Knighthood, St James's Palace, S.W.1.

Madam

I have the honour to inform you that your attendance is required at Buckingham Palace at 10.15 o'clock a.m. (doors open at 9.45 o'clock a.m.) on (date), in order that you, as next of kin, may receive from the King the decoration of the Distinguished Flying Cross conferred on your husband, the late (rank and name), Royal Air Force Volunteer Reserve.

Dress:- Service Dress, Civil Defence Uniform, Morning Dress or dark lounge suit.

You may be accompanied by ***one*** relation only, who must be a blood relation of the deceased (children under seven years of age may not attend) and I shall be glad if you will complete the enclosed form and return it to me immediately. Two third class return railway vouchers will be forwarded to you if you so desire, and I shall be glad if you will give the details required on the form enclosed.

This letter should be produced on entering the Palace as no further cards of admission will be issued.

I am, Madam

Your obedient Servant

Secretary

A considerable number of casualties occurred close to home. Badly damaged aircraft crashed while trying to land and German intruder aircraft accounted for others as they reached apparent safety.

Chadwick, Roy (1893-1947) – Roy Chadwick was born in Farnworth, north west of Manchester, the son of a mechanical engineer. He attended Manchester College of Technology and, very early in life, became fascinated by aircraft, showing enthusiasm for modelling.

As an extremely young man Chadwick was part of the team built up by Alliott Verdon-Roe which developed A V Roe and Co Ltd into a major aircraft manufacturer. Chadwick worked on a range of aircraft during the First World War and designs he was later involved in included the Avro Baby, a very early light aircraft, the Avian, used for record-breaking long distance flights and the Tutor, a key RAF trainer.

Chadwick's contribution to winning the Second World War most famously manifested itself in the designs for the Manchester and Lancaster. He also created the Anson and later the York, Lincoln and Lancastrian emerged from his drawing board.

Roy Dobson, writing in the Oxford Dictionary of National Biography, attributed the quality of genius to Chadwick and suggested that this particularly showed itself, "in an uncanny understanding of the need for perfect control in aeroplanes".

Chadwick was killed, aged 54, on August 23 1947, flying as a passenger in an Avro Tudor, another of his designs, that crashed on a test flight. The aircraft came down at Shirdfold Farm, Adlington, Cheshire, just outside the perimeter of Woodford aerodrome, from which it was taking off. The accident was attributed to a mistake made in servicing and not noticed by the pilot. Ironically 4,040 Lancasters had been assembled at Woodford.

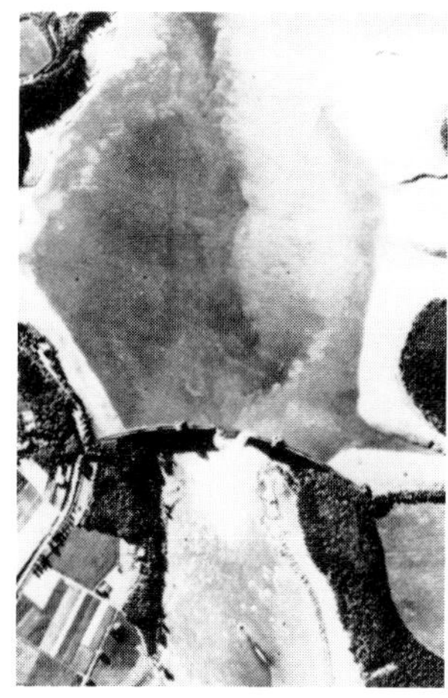

This photograph of the breached Mohne Dam was obtained on the morning after the attack – an illustration of the importance to the bomber offensive of information obtained by photo-reconnaissance aircraft.

Chastise (Operation) – See Dam Busters

Cherwell, Viscount (1886-1957) – Frederick Alexander Lindemann was born while his mother was visiting Germany, though his father had become a naturalised British subject.

Lindemann gained a PhD in Germany and went on to a most distinguished academic career in Britain. During the First World War he worked at the Royal Aircraft Factory, Farnborough, learning to fly and dealing with (at risk to himself) the problems of spin in aircraft. In 1919 he began a long association with Wadham College, Oxford, holding a chair in experimental philosophy, more generally referred to as physics. He was also associated academically with Christ Church, Oxford and lived there for much of his adult life.

Lindemann developed a closer and closer relationship with Winston Churchill and also conceived a concern with the inadequacy of British air defence in the 1930s. Backed by Churchill, Lindemann became a member of the Tizard committee, established by the Air Ministry for the scientific survey of air defence. The committee in that form did not survive stormy relations between Lindemann and Henry Tizard.

With the outbreak of war Lindemann became personal assistant to Churchill at the Admiralty, keeping the same post when Churchill ascended to the Premiership in May 1940.

His influence ranged widely over policy, not least in connection with Bomber Command. He was instrumental in the creation of the Butt Report of 1941, highly damaging to the Command in its assessment of the effectiveness of bomber operations. More positively Lindemann was active in the development of radar systems to assist bombing and was generally an enthusiast for new inventions. He was a proponent of area bombing, but exaggerated its likely effects.

To Churchill and many others Lindemann was "The Prof". He had an abrasive personality, believed in the traditional hierarchy in British life, but often stressed the need to consider the impact of wartime frugality on ordinary people. Great acts of private kindness are attributed to him.

Lindemann was made Baron Cherwell of Oxford in 1941 and became Paymaster General in the following year. In 1943 he was sworn of the Privy Council. He often attended War Cabinet meetings. In the post war era he was Paymaster General again. He became a Companion of Honour in 1953 and Viscount Cherwell in 1956.

Circus – A term for the use of bombers, with heavy fighter escort, being used as bait to bring enemy fighter up to be attacked. It was a tactic that figured in the offensive activity by Fighter Command over the Continent.

Commonwealth War Graves Commission (CWGC) – Founded by Royal Charter as the Imperial War Graves Commission in 1917, with the name being changed to the present one in 1960. The driving force was Fabian Ware (Sir Fabian from 1920) who had been editor of the Morning Post and served with the British Red Cross.

The CWGC has instituted around 2,500 cemeteries and plots around the world for the burial of men and women of British and Commonwealth Forces, as well as many memorials for those who have no known grave.

Simple standard headstones are used, with some design variation according to the nationality of the person or persons in the grave.

Its fundamental principles are:-

Each of the dead should be commemorated by name on the headstone or memorial

Headstones and memorials should be permanent

Headstones should be uniform

There should be no distinction made on account of military or civil rank, race or creed

The Runnymede Memorial, created by the CWGC beside the Thames, was inaugurated by HM The Queen on October 17 1953. On it are the names of RAF aircrew lost during the Second World War, with no known grave, who were based in the UK and countries of northern and eastern

The grave of Pilot Officer Lewis Burpee, DFM, RCAF in Bergen-op-Zoom War Cemetery in The Netherlands. He and his crew died on May 17 1943 flying in "S Sugar", one of the third or reserve wave for the attack on the dams. On the outward flight the aircraft was shot down by flak and caused severe damage at Gilze Rijen airfield when it crashed. Photograph by Gary Godel.

Europe. Those whose bodies were recovered and then formally buried at sea are included.

Designed by Edward Maufe (knighted in 1954 for services to the IWGC), the memorial was built on land donated by Sir Eugen and Lady Millington-Drake. Sir Eugen had played an important part in an early British success of the Second World War. He was Minister to Uruguay at the time of the Battle of the River Plate in December 1939 and had therefore been a key figure in the diplomatic manoeuvring that culminated in the scuttling of the German pocket battleship, *Admiral Graf Spee*.

The graves of many Bomber Command aircrew are cared for by the CWGC across Europe. Often the remains have been removed from their original wartime resting places. Among the places in Germany where CWGC headstones are to be found are Kiel War Cemetery, Berlin 1939-45 War Cemetery, Hanover War Cemetery, Rheinberg War Cemetery and Reichswald Forest War Cemetery.

All CWGC graves and memorials receive regular care. Even those who do not have graves of relatives in the care of the CWGC often find a visit to a cemetery or plot a powerful experience.

Coned – The expression used when an aircraft was caught by a number of enemy searchlights in a co-ordinated action.

"We were just over Holland when we got coned by the searchlights. They were so dazzling you couldn't see a thing.

"There was a blue master light and once that picked you up all the other lights could cone in on you – and oh, was that a naked feeling.

"You were like a black moth caught in the light, expecting the fighters to scream in any moment. They never came."

Wing Commander "Danny" Walker, formerly RCAF, the navigator in Flight Lieutenant Shannon's crew on the Dams raid, quoted in the Daily Mail, April 17 1993 and recalling that operation.

The B-24 ended World War II as the most produced Allied heavy bomber in history with over 18,400 coming off the production line.

Consolidated B-24 Liberator – Though mostly remembered in Britain for its bombing activities with the USAAF, the "Lumbering Lib" also performed various functions in the RAF. As well as flying with Coastal Command, Ferry Command and in the Middle East, the type was operated with electronic jamming equipment by No 223 Squadron in No 100 Group of Bomber Command. Indeed, it was the RAF that coined the name "Liberator".

Although the B-17 Flying Fortress attracted greater fame and was considered more glamorous, the Liberator was produced in much greater numbers.

A prototype of what would become the Liberator first flew on December 29 1939. The first use of the Liberator in a bombing role was by the RAF in the Middle East.

Corkscrew – Violent manoeuvre frequently used to evade night fighters closing in or searchlights – often there would be a shout of "corkscrew" to the pilot from one of the gunners.

Creepback – A tendency to release bombs very shortly before reaching target indicators, leading to bombing further and further back along the bombing run. Human nature was in play here, with a very understandable desire to escape from an area of extreme danger as quickly as possible. Sometimes remarking of the target would be affected by the fires started in the wrong place earlier.

As the problem seemed insoluble, target marking instructions came to take account of likely creepback with the first indicators being dropped ahead of the main target.

Crewing up – Unlike so much else in the services bringing heavy bomber crews together was a haphazard business. Many remember standing in a hangar with many other men of differing trades and being told to sort themselves into crews. Sometimes the process took a little longer, but it still usually came down to who you stood next to or liked the look of, or who somebody you had found already knew, or whether you had a preference for flying with officers or NCOs.

Dam Busters (Operation Chastise) – On the night of May 16/17 1943 No 617 Squadron, specially formed and trained for the purpose, flew into action for the first time. Its task, under the name of Operation Chastise, was to attack the dams of western Germany.

The Lancasters ("Type 464 Provisioning Lancaster") that the squadron used were adapted to take the mines, codenamed "Upkeep" and about to enter popular imagination as "bouncing bombs". These mines were also specifically designed for such a target. Another modification to the aircraft was the removal of the mid upper turret to save weight, so one air gunner flew in the front turret.

There should have been 21 Lancasters taking part in the operation, but illness and problems with aircraft availability reduced this on the night to 19, of which 11 returned to Scampton. Of the missing aircrew, 53 had been killed and three had become PoWs.

The night's work resulted in the destruction of the Mohne and Eder dams, damage to the Sorpe and (officially) to the Ennepe, though the historian John Sweetman has argued that the dam hit by Flight Sergeant Townsend's mine was in fact probably the Bever.

Consideration had first been given by the Air Ministry to the dams as a target in 1937, though much hesitation and debate ensued. Later Barnes Wallis of Vickers was the key figure in producing the weapon that was used.

Wing Commander Guy Gibson (centre) with fellow Dam Busters.

No 617 Squadron was not formed, in No 5 Group, until March 17 1943, exactly two months before conditions would be ideal for the attack. The much decorated Wing Commander Guy Gibson, who had been CO of No 106 Squadron, was appointed to form and lead 617. He quickly put together a group of aircrew, some of whom were already known to him, some were highly experienced and others far less so. Indeed, contrary to the story as it was later presented, there were men for whom the dams attack was their first operation. Training was intense, including much flying over suitable British dams, such as the Derwent in Derbyshire.

Chastise achieved disruption to the German war effort, though not as much as had been hoped for. The dams were rebuilt and it was a surprise to the Germans that further attacks were not attempted by the RAF while this work was in progress.

The success which was achieved nonetheless presented the British authorities with a considerable propaganda coup and the opportunity was grasped, including by Winston Churchill, the Prime Minister, who, on May 19, addressing the American Congress in Washington DC, made reference to the raid. Photographs obtained by aerial reconnaissance had already appeared in British and American newspapers when he spoke.

On May 25 34 "immediate" awards for aircrew on Chastise were gazetted, a remarkable number for a small operation. These decorations were the VC for Gibson, DSOs for five pilots (Flight Lieutenants J C McCarthy, D J H Maltby, H B Martin and D J Shannon and Pilot Officer L G Knight), CGMs for two NCO pilots (Flight Sergeant K W Brown and Flight Sergeant W C Townsend), four bars to the DFC, 10 DFCs, one bar to the DFM and 11 DFMs.

The King and Queen visited Scampton on May 27 and met participants and those decorated attended an investiture at Buckingham Palace on June 22, at which 617's decorations were presented (by The Queen) before those for all others present.

No 617 Squadron remained in being as a "special" squadron. Targets attacked after the dams included the *Tirpitz*, the V weapon facilities at Siracourt in France, a railway tunnel near Saumur (to delay German forces moving forward after D Day), the Gnome & Rhone aero engine factory at Limoges, U-boat pens at the Dutch port of Ijmuiden and the Dortmund Ems Canal.

"Let me know when you are ready; and remember, not a word to anyone. This is just an ordinary new squadron. Secrecy is vital." – Air Vice-Marshal Cochrane, AO C-in-C No 5 Group, in telling Wing Commander Gibson that he was to form No 617 Squadron, as quoted by Gibson in *Enemy Coast Ahead.*

"Op No 14 via Holland to the Hun. Satisfactory attack on the Eder dam 18 miles west of Kassel. Average ht 100 feet." The assault on the dams as recorded in the logbook of Flight Sergeant Len Sumpter, the bomb aimer in Flight Lieutenant Shannon's Lancaster. Sumpter received the DFM.

In 1951 the book *The Dam Busters* by Paul Brickhill, added gloss to the legend, describing the formation of No 617 Squadron and the attack on the dams, to the extent that was then permitted by security considerations. Brickhill was an Australian journalist and fighter pilot who had been shot down and taken prisoner in North Africa in 1943.

Four years later a black and white film of the same name appeared which was based both on Brickhill's book and on *Enemy Coast Ahead* written by Guy Gibson. The accompanying march was composed by Eric Coates. In later years the film has generally been referred to as *The Dambusters.*

Stars of the film included, Richard Todd as Guy Gibson, Michael Redgrave as Barnes Wallis and Basil Sydney as Sir Arthur Harris. Other well known actors to take part included Ursula Jeans, Robert Shaw, Richard Leech, Hugh Manning, Derek Farr, Raymond Huntley, Charles Carson, Bill Kerr, Ewan Solon and John Fraser. The script was written by R C Sherriff whose oft performed play *Journey's End* (1928) was based on the letters he wrote home from the trenches of the First World War.

Inevitably the film was affected by the continuing secrecy over some aspects of the attack and contained historical inaccuracies. However, both film and music achieved enormous and continuing impact. The film was remastered in 2007 and a new version was in preparation in early 2011.

"He was a young man of great physical and mental courage, allied to determination and stubbornness. He was a brilliant pilot but reckoned to be overshadowed in this respect by (his dams raid colleague) 'Mickey' Martin. He was a born leader of men but not entirely popular with those who served with him, since he was quite cold and calculating and inclined to be very 'cocky'. He was extremely ambitious both professionally and personally and yet very protective towards his subordinates. Had he survived the war he would have had a highly successful career in the RAF." Richard Todd (a former officer in The King's Own Yorkshire Light Infantry and The Parachute Regiment) gives an actor's perspective in a letter dated June 8 1995 to a 12-year-old schoolboy undertaking a project on Guy Gibson.

The DFC.

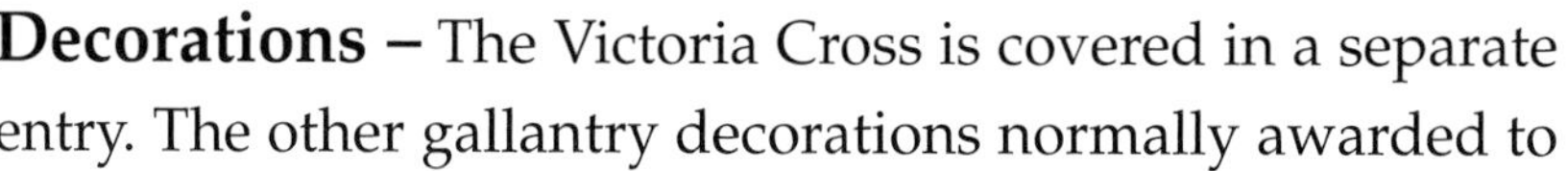

Decorations – The Victoria Cross is covered in a separate entry. The other gallantry decorations normally awarded to

Bomber Command aircrew during the Second World War were, for officers, the Distinguished Service Order (DSO), with the Distinguished Flying Cross (DFC) and the Air Force Cross (AFC) for officers and warrant officers. Other ranks awards were the Conspicuous Gallantry Medal (CGM), the Distinguished Flying Medal (DFM) and the Air Force Medal (AFM).

The DSO.

The DSO was instituted in 1886 and involved admission to an order; until the early years of the First World War some awards were made for services not performed under fire. At its institution it was available to officers in both the Royal Navy and Army – a revised Royal Warrant approved on April 1 1918 extended the award to the newly-formed RAF. As a gallantry decoration the DSO ranked immediately below the VC.

At the beginning of the Second World War there was no decoration for RAF other ranks at the second level, that is between the VC and the DFM, unlike the Royal Navy which had the CGM and the Army which had the Distinguished Conduct Medal (DCM). To make good this deficiency a Royal Warrant of November 10 1942 extended the CGM to other ranks of the Army and the RAF for deeds, "whilst flying in active operations against the enemy".

The DFC was instituted by a Royal Warrant of June 3 1918, just over two months after the formation of the RAF. This warrant also established the DFM, AFC and AFM. The AFC and the AFM were awarded for courage or devotion to duty while flying, but not during operations against the enemy.

The DFC and the DFM were awarded for an act or acts of valour, courage or devotion to duty performed, "whilst flying in active operations against the enemy". The awards were equivalent to the Royal Navy's Distinguished Service Cross (DSC) and Distinguished Service Medal (DSM) and the Army's Military Cross (MC) and Military Medal (MM). Other ranks sometimes received the British Empire Medal (BEM) for gallant acts.

Some RAF personnel who performed gallant acts, not in the air, received Royal Navy and Army awards.

Following a fundamental review of the system for gallantry awards, instigated by the then Prime Minister, John Major, in 1993, the DFM and AFM, together with the other service equivalents ceased to be awarded and all ranks became eligible for those previously awarded only to officers and warrant officers.

In the 1993 changes the second level awards of all three services were replaced by the Conspicuous Gallantry Cross (CGC), with the DSO reserved for outstanding leadership and service on military operations.

de Havilland Mosquito – "The Wooden Wonder" came from a pre-war private venture by de Havilland. Despite the glory heaped on the Mosquito in later years, the initial response from the Air Ministry was unenthusiastic.

Armourers check the bomb load for Mosquitos of No 105 Squadron at RAF Marham.

de Havilland Mosquito B Mk IVs of No 105 Squadron based at RAF Marham in 1942.

An order was placed in March 1940, but even then other matters took priority. Eventually the first flight took place on November 25 1940. The official mind began to see the advantages of a bomber that could manoeuvre like a fighter.

Sir Arthur Harris was another who was not initially a fan of the concept. He suggested that the Mosquito might be regarded by history in the same light as the Fairey Battle in which so many RAF aircrew had died early in the war.

The first version of the Mosquito to enter operational service was for photo-reconnaissance, with bombers following for No 2 Group, the first going to No 105 Squadron at Swanton Morley, Norfolk. They went into action for the first time as a follow up to the 1,000 bomber attack on Cologne at the end of May 1942.

The Mosquito carried a crew of two who perhaps needed to be fairly slim to escape in a hurry through the hatch in the floor. A navigator described how watching his pilot climb aboard brought to mind a Victorian child sweeping chimneys. The aircraft had two Rolls Royce Merlin engines, carried cannon and machine guns and up to 2,000lb of bombs. Despite the use of wood the aircraft proved to be able to withstand considerable punishment.

Other major roles for the "Mossie" were as a fighter bomber and night fighter. Including aircraft built in Canada and Australia, 7,781 were produced. The last left RAF operational service in 1955. The type was also operated by the Canadian, Australian, New Zealand, South African and United States Air Forces.

Dominion and Other Overseas Air Forces – The air forces of Canada, Australia, New Zealand and South Africa in particular contributed on a major scale to the operations of Bomber Command in the Second World War.

The Royal Australian Air Force (RAAF) was the largest and dated back to a proposal put to the Australian government in 1918 by Major General J G Legge that an air service should be formed. The date of formation is considered to be March 31 1921.

Sergeant Jimmy Ward VC, Royal New Zealand Air Force. He was born at Wanganui in the country's North Island. Shortly after this photograph was taken he was lost over Hamburg.

A key factor in the establishment of the RAAF was the donation by the British government of 128 aircraft, under a plan that came to be known as the "Imperial Gift" and also included a wide range of other vital equipment including spares, hangars, radios, tools, motor vehicles and bombs. Other Air Forces benefitted from this scheme.

The Royal Canadian Air Force (RCAF) was officially established on April 1 1924, though there had been two previous Canadian air arms. In 1968, all three Canadian armed services were brought together and the RCAF ceased to exist in independent form.

Formed in 1923, the Royal New Zealand Air Force (RNZAF) now operates under the umbrella of the New Zealand Defence Force. Though at the outbreak of the Second World War the RNZAF was small and equipped with obsolete aircrafts preparations had been made for the coming conflict. For example, a reserve of volunteers had been established that received elementary flying training through aero clubs and provided pilots for both the RNZAF and the RAF.

South Africa appointed a Director of Air Services in 1920 and the title, South African Air Force (SAAF) was used from February 1 1923.

At the outbreak of the Second World War the Southern Rhodesian Air Unit became an Air Force and was absorbed into the RAF in 1940.

The Indian Air Force operated under RAF direction and many Indians flew with the RAF.

A number of squadrons that flew in Bomber Command became nominally part of the Dominion air forces, though still under the control of the RAF. There was much behind the scenes negotiation on this point, aimed, as far as the RAF was concerned, at ensuring that Dominion aircrew were not drained away too quickly for service in their native countries and theatres in which those countries were heavily involved.

Many RAF personnel during the war wore the insignia of other air forces and countries including Poland, Czechoslovakia, Free French, The Netherlands, Norway, Belgium, the United States, Denmark and Turkey. In some cases RAF squadrons were nominally part of the overseas air force.

In 2010 a Second World War Bomber Command squadron was re-formed by the Royal Australian Air Force. The announcement of the decision to re-create No 460 Squadron came during a commemorative service to mark the 89th anniversary of the founding of the RAAF.

The Polish Air Force Memorial on the edge of RAF Northolt in west London. The names of Polish airmen lost while flying from British airfields are inscribed on it. "They lived with us and died with us in all the battles in the war...," wrote Viscount Trenchard appealing after the war for funds to build the memorial.

The squadron was intended to operate in the defence imagery and geospatial sphere, including analysis of imagery and other information to describe, evaluate and depict physical features and geographically referenced activities.

No 460 Squadron was formed at RAF Molesworth (Cambridgeshire) on November 15 1941 and operated with Wellingtons. It later received Halifaxs and then Lancasters and flew from Breighton, Binbrook and East Kirkby.

According to the website of the Australian War Memorial, "The squadron is regarded as having been the most efficient of the Australian bomber squadrons. It maintained consistently higher serviceability rates among its aircraft, set numerous operational records within Bomber Command, flew the most bombing raids of any Australian squadron, and was credited with the greatest tonnage of bombs dropped – 24,856 tons. The Australian War Memorial's Lancaster G for George was a 460 Squadron aircraft. The squadron, however, suffered heavily. It lost 181 aircraft on operations and suffered 1,018 fatal casualties (589 Australian) – the highest number of any of the Australian squadrons."

"Several thousand Australians joined the RAAF during World War II and went to a war so far away from their home and loved ones. They came from the land, from sheep stations, factories, offices, cities, country towns, and brought with them that unique sense of humour and devoted mateship that is the fierce pride of the Australian Warrior.

"The Runnymede Memorial in England commemorates over 4,000 Australian aviators who paid the ultimate price to win that war. This is a disturbing figure, not only by its magnitude but by its obscurity. Many Australians today are not aware of the thousands of young Australian men who took part in the Battles in the Skies over Europe during WWII, one of Australia's greatest and deadliest commitments to battle."

From the website dedicated to Nos 463 and 467 Squadrons.

"As I write the last of the men of the Royal Australian Air Force are going home from Europe. Thousands of them have already returned to civilian life in Australia.

"Each of these men will carry home his own memories of service overseas, his own fund of reminiscence relating to what in most cases must have been the most vivid span of his lifetime. His friends will hear some of these memories; mostly they will be the lighter, humorous type of tale airmen delight in telling – stories against themselves, against their service friends. Those at home will hear little from him of the grimmer side of operational life in the war against Fortress Europe, of the daily dangers of that great battle, of personal acts of courage and heroism ——-

"The book will be read with interest not only in Australia but in thousands of homes in Britain into which the men of the RAAF went as strangers and left as friends during those six years in Europe."

Air Vice-Marshal H N Wrigley, Air Officer Commanding RAAF Overseas Headquarters, Foreword to *RAAF Over Europe*, 1946.

Douglas Boston – One of the less remembered types to see service in Bomber Command, the Boston lll was nonetheless used by a number of squadrons in No 2 Group. It was a twin-engined light bomber, usually with a crew of three and carrying a bomb load of up to 4,000lb. Known as the Havoc, the type also saw service with the RAF as an intruder and night fighter. It was also used by the USAAF and by a number of other Air Forces.

Some Vichy French examples went into action against the Allies during Operation Torch, the invasion of French territory in North Africa.

Douglas Boston Mk IV.

Dresden – Since the end of the Second World War the word "Dresden" has entered common parlance to the point where it is sometimes used as a synonym for "terrible act of war". It is difficult to understand why the capital of Saxony, frightful though the firestorm it suffered was, should be chosen ahead of Coventry, Hamburg, Tokyo and a range of other targets. The scale of attacks varied, as well as the number of casualties and the technology available to be used but there seems no difference in principle.

In 1945 a number of co-ordinated attacks were carried out on Dresden by the RAF and USAAF, notably on the night of February 13/14 1945, when almost 800 RAF bombers were involved. This was quickly followed by an attack mounted by 331 bombers of the USAAF.

Most of the legends associated with "Dresden" can be shown to be untrue:-

■ Up to that point it had escaped bombing.

Previous attacks had been mounted, including that by the USAAF on October 7 1944, when Dresden was a secondary target to the oil refinery at Ruhland.

■ The target was personally chosen by Air Chief Marshal Harris.

The intention to attack Dresden as a target was discussed at the highest levels of the British, American and Russian governments. The historian Martin Gilbert has described the attack as a direct result of the Yalta Conference of Allied leaders. Churchill, as Prime Minister, was demanding such action.

■ Dresden had no military importance.

Frederick Taylor in his book Dresden points to a document issued by the weapons office of the German High Command in 1944 and listing 127 factories in Dresden with their own code for military secrecy. There were many manufacturing units in addition to that. Further, Dresden was a major transportation centre and contained many German soldiers destined to seek to stem the Russian advance. Dresden was also one of the cities that the

Germans planned to fortify so that the Russian advance could be resisted street by street.

■ Several hundred thousand people died in the 1945 raids.

Most modern historians put the figure at between 25,000 and 30,000.

A strong case can be made for saying that perhaps it was not necessary to attack the city so late in the war, though the men who ordered the attack did not have the knowledge available now of how close the end of the war was. Many would argue too (including some of the aircrew who took part) that it was wrong to place the aiming point in the centre of the city when most of the factories were in the suburbs.

The point remains that most of the criticisms of the attacks on Dresden are criticisms of bombing as a form of warfare carried out in the Second World War by all the major powers.

"When people ask me if I have sympathy for the people of Dresden I say, 'When the people of Dresden show sympathy for the people of Coventry then I will return that sympathy.'" RAF veteran speaking in 2009.

"As I flew across the city it was very obvious to me that there was a large number of black and white half timbered buildings; it reminded me of Shropshire and Hereford and Ludlow." An airmen remembers one impression from the attack.

Early Returns – A phrase describing crews who turned back before reaching the target – more colloquially these were "boomerangs". The reasons for returning could be genuine, for instance severe damage or mechanical malfunction, but there could also be varying degrees of lameness about the reasons given. COs were on the lookout for a pattern of weak reasons developing.

Emergency Landing Grounds – Airfields near the coast that could be used by crippled aircraft unable to regain their home station.

Empire Air Training Scheme – Scheme established in 1940 under which potential Bomber Command and other RAF aircrew were trained. Countries in which schools were established under the scheme included Canada, Australia, South Africa, Rhodesia and the United States.

Evasion and Escape – Many Bomber Command personnel shot down over the Continent, either avoided capture or were captured and later escaped. They were aided by civilians in all the occupied countries, sometimes as individuals and in other instances operating as part of organised escape lines. Often the object was to reach a neutral country.

"Battledress wasn't normally allowed in London, but we'd been given a special permit should we be questioned by the military police.

"London looked wonderful. The streets were filled with people on their way to work and I looked into the faces of passers-by as I walked by them. These people were free and had always been free. They didn't know the daily fears of ordinary people living in Holland, Belgium and France. They could travel where they pleased without fear of being stopped. They had no need to produce identity papers all the time. They could speak freely and could still criticise the government if they so wished. As I walked along I wondered if they knew just how fortunate they were."

Pilot Officer (later Flight Lieutenant) Bob Kellow, RAAF, remembers, in his book, *Paths to Freedom,* returning to England, three months after he baled out over the Netherlands in September 1943. He was the wireless operator in the crew of Flight Lieutenant Les Knight, RAAF, of No 617 Squadron, during an attack on the Dortmund-Ems Canal. Five aircraft were lost.

After hitting trees the aircraft flew on for about an hour before Knight ordered the crew to abandon the aircraft. All his seven comrades (an extra Air Gunner was being carried) survived, but Les Knight died as he tried to land the stricken Lancaster near Den Ham. It hit a bank and exploded. A memorial has since been placed at the scene.

Extracts from the Speech by the then Chief of the Air Staff Air Chief Marshal Sir Michael Graydon at the Royal Air Force Escaping Society Gala Dinner at RAF Cranwell, September 1995.

"I am delighted to be your guest tonight. It is over a year ago that Sir Lewis Hodges asked if I would attend: the event has been etched into my diary since: I would not have missed it for anything.

"I count it a particular honour to have been invited to be with you tonight on your 50th anniversary, both a commemoration, a celebration and a poignant end of a particular chapter in your remarkable history.

"You are one of the most exclusive and extraordinary societies in the world, a Society not only brought about to repay a debt but with the aim, I have no doubt, inspired by a deep and often very personal desire, to maintain contact with the families of those who had literally laid down their lives for others in the pursuit of freedom.

"Thus Lord Portal's directive in 1945 for the RAF Escaping Society to maintain links with the 'Helpers' has been carried out with a dedication and diligence which would be hard to match. I would venture to suggest that he would be well pleased both in the manner in which these links have been maintained and in the strength, still after 50 years, of this Escaping Society.

"But perhaps there should be no surprise, for as members of this remarkable Society, you have had some unique characteristics, a combination of courage, determination, cunning, imagination and no doubt some luck.

"Have you ever thought of going into politics?!

"For whatever reason, for whatever aspect of character carried you through, you escaped, you evaded and you returned. That is an entrance test unique to any society.

"And yet, of course, you would be the first to acknowledge that none of this would have been possible without the Helpers. And you above all would know that, however long it took to reach safety, whether it was days, weeks or even months, there was an end game and when you reached it, God willing, you would be free.

"For your Helpers, that was not the case. They had everything to lose, their family, their home and overshadowing it, the persistent fear, the threat of concentration camps and execution – a pressure that was there for years. I can understand why you feel so strongly and have committed yourselves so valiantly to the links with the Helpers.

"With over 2,800 British and Commonwealth airmen making it back to the United Kingdom, the number of Helpers was vast... Let me, on behalf of today's Royal Air Force, pay tribute to you and to all those to whom we owe so much.

"Now you have decided to close the Society. If I may say so, you have done it with great good sense and with much dignity.

"You were set a task by Lord Portal 50 years ago. As one of his successors I can say you have met fully the remit placed on you then. Today's Royal Air Force is honoured to take part in this occasion and salutes each one of you tonight."

See also entry for Internment.

Exodus (Operation) – Before VE Day Bomber Command began flights to bring released PoWs home from Europe and they continued after the end of hostilities. Though not without accident and loss these flights ensured that men of all three services reached home much quicker than many of their counterparts in 1918.

f

Fairey Battle – When the Fairey Battle day bomber first flew in March 1936 it seemed rather a modern design. By the outbreak of the Second World War it was obsolete and suffered terribly in action in 1939 and 1940, particularly while operating in the Advanced Air Striking Force.

Powered by Rolls Royce Merlin engines, the Battle carried a crew of three – pilot, bomb aimer/observer and wireless operator/air gunner – and had a maximum speed of 257 mph. The bomb load was 1,000lb.

The first RAF victory of the war was claimed by AC1 J E Summers flying in a Battle of No 103 Squadron on September 27 1939. He received the DFM after he shot down a Messerschmitt Bf 109 flown by Gefrieter Joseph Scherm who was killed.

However, three days later, the limitations of the Battle were amply demonstrated. Six aircraft of No 150 Squadron were sent on a reconnaissance over Germany, one experienced engine trouble and four were shot down by Bf 109s. The aircraft flown by Squadron Leader W M L MacDonald crashed on return to the airfield at Ecury-sur-Coole, south east of Reims and both his crew members, Sergeant F H Gardiner and AC1 A Murcar were injured and burned. They eventually received the DFC, BEM and DFM respectively.

On May 13 1940, three days into the Blitzkreig, No 12 Squadron was asked to provide volunteers to attack bridges over the Albert Canal in the vicinity of Maastricht. Six aircraft

Pilot and crew ready to board their Fairey Battle aircraft with No 218 Squadron in 1940.

took off and one returned. Posthumous VCs, the first air VCs of the war, went to Flying Officer Donald Garland and Sergeant Tom Gray, pilot and navigator of the leading aircraft in the first wave.

An official account referred to "the devoted heroism displayed by the crews in undertaking a virtually suicidal task".

May 14 was a further terrible day for the Battle squadrons with 30 aircraft becoming casualties.

Battles remained operational in Bomber Command for some months after the fall of France, but the main roles of the aircraft quickly became training and target towing.

Some of the men who flew the Battle into action were inclined to regard it as "The Flying Coffin".

FIDO – Thanks in large part to Clean Air Acts of Parliament in 1956 and 1968, fog in 21st century Britain is far less of a problem than it was in the Second World War. FIDO was developed at Birmingham University as a means of dispersing fog at airfields to enable aircraft to land. The letters are often said to stand for Fog Interpretation and Dispersal Operation, though there are other suggestions.

"One of the longest flights was to the synthetic oil plant at Politz. There was fog at Coningsby and we were surprised that the operation wasn't scrubbed. On return we were sent to nearby Metheringham, which was equipped with FIDO fog dispersion. Burning hundreds of gallons of fuel along the runway to disperse the fog was expensive and we couldn't keep them hanging about, but when I made a run at 500 ft all I could see was an orange glow. So I made a run at 250 ft and this time we could just make out the runway. We landed off the third circuit. Then we discovered that someone had missed the runway and crashed into a wood alongside, the crew being killed. The burning Lancaster had set fire to the wood, covering the area with smoke, which FIDO was not designed to disperse!" Group Captain Peter Johnson, quoted in *So Many*.

Flight Engineer – In the heavy bombers Flight Engineers replaced the former second pilots. They monitored the performance of the aircraft during an operation, not least matters connected with the engines. Though most were not trained as pilots it would often be the Flight Engineer who took over the controls from a wounded pilot or to give an exhausted skipper a rest.

Freeman Air Chief Marshal Sir Wilfrid Rhodes Bt (1888-1953) – Attended Rugby School and Royal Military College Sandhurst before serving in The Manchester Regiment. He obtained his pilot's licence in 1913 and became a member of the Royal Flying Corps, going to France in August 1914 with No 2 Squadron.

During the Battle of Mons a defect in his aircraft forced him down behind enemy lines. He evaded capture and returned to his squadron, swimming the River Aisne in the process – a very early example of evasion by an airman.

Freeman moved to No 9 Squadron and earned an MC during the Battle of Neuve Chapelle; he would later be appointed to the DSO. He became an instructor in England, commanded No 14 Squadron in Egypt and led Wings in France. In 1919 Freeman received a permanent commission as a Wing Commander. He held a number of training appointments, including command of the Central Flying School at Upavon. He was Air Officer Commanding Trans-Jordan and Palestine 1930-33.

From 1934-36, as an Air Vice-Marshal, Freeman was Commandant of the RAF Staff College, Andover. In 1936 he joined the Air Council as Air Member, Research and Development. In this post his responsibilities included finding new types of aircraft and other equipment and ensuring the development of those projects already underway.

Freeman was promoted to Air Marshal and had aircraft production added to his responsibilities. His title became Air Member for Development and Production and he was now a key figure in providing the means of Britain going to war.

When the Ministry of Aircraft Production was created after Churchill became Prime Minister in May 1940 Freeman found himself reporting to Lord Beaverbrook. At this time he was promoted to Air Chief Marshal. Clashes between two strong personalities were inevitable, though Beaverbrook spoke warmly of Freeman.

From November 1940 Freeman was Vice Chief of the Air Staff, relieving Air Chief Marshal Portal of many administrative duties. Freeman retired from the RAF in 1942 and became Chief Executive of the Ministry of Aircraft Production. It was a post very much to his taste and he held it until 1945.

Fringe Merchants – Crews with the habit of dropping their bombs before the aiming point was reached, thus eliminating some of the danger (and effectiveness) of a raid.

Gardening – Minelaying operations.

GEE – Early form of radar to assist bomber navigation. The aircraft using the system needed to pick up pulses transmitted by ground stations. GEE was introduced in 1942 and provided an immediate improvement in navigation. Various security activities (including references to a fictitious system called "Jay") meant that it was some time before the enemy developed counter measures.

Grand Slam – A larger version of the Tallboy bomb (see separate entry), weighing 22,000lb and closer to the size that Barnes Wallis envisaged when he conceived the idea of "earthquake" bombs. The Grand Slam followed the Tallboy into service.

The first Grand Slam to be dropped on an operation was that released by Squadron Leader C C Calder of No 617 Squadron over the Schildesche Viaduct, near Bielefeld in Eastern Westphalia on March 14 1945. Tallboys followed and the earthquake effect brought down a considerable portion of the structure.

It seems that Calder's place in history was only secured after a piece of quick thinking. The then CO of No 617 Squadron, Wing Commander J B Fauquier was also due to carry a Grand Slam on the attack. Paul Brickhill in *The Dam Busters* recorded that just before take off Fauquier's Lancaster suffered the failure of its starboard inner engine. Intent on commandeering Calder's aircraft the CO sprinted across the airfield, but Calder realised the turn of events and hurriedly took off.

Groundcrew – Bomber Command groundcrew spent much of their time working on aircraft in the open whatever the weather might throw at them. Many have claimed that they deserved more recognition than they received.

Aircraft had about 10 groundcrew of various trades allocated to them. There was usually an early morning start and a complete inspection of the aircraft lasting about three hours.

"Keep them flying at all costs was the motto of the groundcrew, but on occasions this was carried to the extreme. When the engines of a Lancaster were run up before taxying to the runway it was found that one bank of six spark plugs needed changing. To have waited for the engines to cool down would have meant the aircraft being too late to take off.

"A fitter, without a thought, put his hands into the hot engine and changed the plugs. He was severely burned, but the aircraft took off on time."

Alan Cooper writing in *RAF News*, 2002.

A Stirling of No 7 Squadron is bombed up at Oakington

At the end of the war Air Chief Marshal Harris argued passionately, but unsuccessfully, that the role of the ground personnel of Bomber Command should have been recognised with an award.

Group – The second tier of RAF command structure, providing the functions of operational command and control.

At the start of the war Bomber Command contained Nos 1, 2, 3, 4 and 5 Groups. No 1 Group became, in effect, the Advanced Air Striking Force in France for a time before resuming its previous role. No 2 Group, consisting of light bombers, suffered very heavy losses in the early days of the war. On June 1 1943 No 2 Group left Bomber Command, to become part of the 2nd Tactical Air Force, although two Mosquito squadrons remained with Bomber Command.

No 6 Group was re-established on January 1 1943 and was part of the Royal Canadian Air Force. No 8 Group was the Pathfinder Force from January 1943. No 100 Group for special duties was formed on December 3 1943.

Proposals to set up Australian and New Zealand Groups were not put into effect.

Guinea Pig Club – The Club was founded in June 1941 at the Queen Victoria Hospital, East Grinstead, Sussex by RAF aircrew who were undergoing reconstructive plastic surgery (not always as a result of burns) under the direction of the New Zealand plastic surgeon Archibald McIndoe, who was knighted in 1960.

The name of the club indicated the innovative nature of McIndoe's work and drinking played a large part in early activities, with beer being provided as part of McIndoe's regime. However membership of what its members regarded as an elite institution gave access to mutual support that would last a lifetime.

Amongst the Guinea Pigs who gained some celebrity was Bill Foxley, who had been the navigator of a Wellington at an Operational Training Unit that crashed on take off in 1944. Foxley escaped unhurt, but went back into the burning wreckage and dragged the wireless operator clear, although he later died. In the rescue Foxley suffered terrible burns, lost one eye and had the other badly damaged. He was in hospital for three and a half years.

In 1969 Bill Foxley appeared in a small, but oft remembered, role in the film *The Battle of Britain*, depicting a burned pilot introduced to the WAAF officer played by Susannah York.

After the war Foxley worked for the Central Electricity Generating Board, took up long distance running, was a founder of a disablement charity, encouraged those badly burned in later conflicts and raised money for the Blond McIndoe Research Foundation.

Another of the indomitable breed of Guinea Pigs was Colin Ward, as a 27 year old Sergeant pilot, the skipper of a Wellington of No 101 Squadron on the night of March 9/10 1942, flying from Bourn to attack Essen.

As the aircraft left the target area it was hit by anti-aircraft fire. Ward was badly wounded in the head and believed that he had been partially blinded – actually part of his scalp was hanging down over one eye. Despite having only one engine, no instruments or hydraulics and with the front turret and wireless out of action he determined to do all he could to reach home. He did offer his crew the chance to bale out, but they refused to leave him.

The stricken Wellington reached Bourn but, with an obstruction on the airfield, was diverted to Oakington, where Ward decided to land off the runway to avoid blocking it. This led to a collision with another aircraft that had already crash-landed. Sergeant Ward was further injured and then badly burned before he could escape.

He received an immediate DFM and was in hospital for two years. It was Archie McIndoe himself who told him that his flying career was over.

Colin Ward spent most of his post war career in insurance and in his last years was quite relaxed about telling his story if asked, though around the anniversary of that night over Essen he would often suffer nightmares. His big regret was that his logbook disappeared during his spell in hospital.

We are McIndoe's Army
We are his Guinea Pigs
With dermatomes and pedicles
Glass eyes, false teeth and wigs
And when we get our discharge
We'll shout with all our might
"Per Ardua Ad Astra
We'd rather drink than fight"

John Hunter runs the gas works,
Ross Tilley wields the knife.
And if they are not careful
They'll have your flaming life.
So, Guinea Pigs, stand steady
For all your surgeon's calls:
And if their hands aren't steady
They'll whip off both your ears

We've had some mad Australians,
Some French, some Czechs, some Poles
We've even had some Yankees,
God bless their precious souls.
While as for the Canadians –
Ah! That's a different thing.
They couldn't stand our accent
And built a separate Wing

Three verses of *The Guinea Pig Anthem*, normally sung to *Aurelia* by Samuel Sebastian Wesley, often associated with the hymn, *The Church's One Foundation* by Samuel John Stone. Other vital members of the McIndoe team were the surgeon Percy Jayes and Sister Jill Mullins.

"Foxley had to overcome very public horror of his scarred features. Commuting daily by train from Crawley to London, the seat next to his often remained empty. Passengers who moved to take up the seat would change their minds at the last moment, prompting Foxley to tell them:- 'It's all right. I'm not going to bite you.'" From the obituary of Bill Foxley published in The Daily Telegraph, December 16 2010.

"Archie generated a bond of fellowship in which rank was forgotten. He believed that nothing should stand in the way of making terribly mutilated human beings whole again and so we had much more freedom than was traditional in military or medical circles.

"Local people had to get used to the sight of us walking out to the pubs in the evenings, those who were lame or in wheelchairs assisted by those whose worst problem might be a considerably re-arranged face. Archie wanted to boost our confidence and help us achieve our common ambition to get back into the war. He invited us into the operating theatre to watch him at work and it was there that we began to mutter 'guinea pig.'" Group Captain Tom Gleave, a fighter pilot who was first Vice-President of the club, speaking in 1992.

H2S – A ground mapping system carried in aircraft and therefore not limited in its range. It was first used in an attack on Hamburg in January 1943.

Hamburg – Weather conditions had prevented Hamburg becoming one of the targets for the Thousand Bomber raids in 1942. In July and August 1943 four attacks by Bomber Command, with two from the USAAF, devastated much of the major city, port and naval centre, causing perhaps 45,000 deaths. Overall, the attacks were known as Operation Gomorrah.

Much of the remaining population fled the city and there was a significant morale effect on German commanders and the German people. Albert Speer, armaments minister, was quoted as saying that six similar attacks could end the war in the allies' favour. In fact Hamburg was closer to England than many of the other potential targets and was extremely easy to identify and mark. The capacity did not exist to bring Speer's worst fears to pass.

The awful Hamburg firestorm that has, in particular, gone down in history was created by the second RAF attack and the weather conditions of that night.

Handley Page Halifax – Developed from an Air Ministry specification for a two-engined bomber, the Halifax, with four engines would become one of the mainstays of the

Halifax

The local memorial near Antwerp to the crew of a Halifax of No 51 Squadron that crashed after being attacked by a night fighter during an operation to Cologne on the night of June 28/29 1943. The captain, Pilot Officer John Tay was killed along with Sergeant Smith, Sergeant Redshaw, Pilot Officer Houlston, Sergeant Butler and Sergeant Vidal, RCAF. Sergeant Eldridge, the second pilot, evaded capture and Pilot Officer Popley (navigator) became a PoW.
Photographs by Fik Geuens.

Bomber Command assault on Germany. It would also be deployed in transport, maritime reconnaissance, anti-submarine, glider tug and air ambulance roles. The first flight of a prototype occurred six weeks after the outbreak of war.

Halifax 1s began to enter service with No 35 Squadron towards the end of 1940. The squadron flew the first Halifax operational sorties to Le Havre in March 1941. Increased fuel capacity and the addition of a dorsal turret were features of the Mk ll, however performance suffered and later Mk lls were modified including the removal of the nose turret.

Further improvements, including the use of Bristol Hercules radial engines (originally power was provided by Rolls Royce Merlins) were achieved in the Mk lll, which entered squadron service from February 1944.

Initially Air Chief Marshal Harris was unenthusiastic about the Mk lll, claiming that it was not clearly better than its predecessors and that production should be concentrated on Lancasters.

Many aircrew who flew in the "Halibag" regarded it with affection – praising the Lancaster to the exclusion of the

A Halifax Bomber of No 35 Squadron, 1941.

The silhouette of a Halifax over Leipzig, February 1944.

Halifax at gatherings of veterans is rather akin to talking endlessly about the Spitfire and overlooking the Hurricane when "fighter boys" are assembled.

Two Hampden crews immediately after their return from attacking German naval units.

Handley Page Hampden – The Hampden emerged from an Air Ministry specification of 1932, calling for a twin-engined bomber, that, perhaps surprisingly, was also the procreator of the rather different Vickers Wellington.

Equipped with Bristol Pegasus radial piston engines and normally carrying a crew of four, the Hampden could carry 4,000lb of bombs. It had a maximum speed of just over 250 mph. There were twin forward firing 0.303in machine guns and further guns of the same type in ventral and dorsal positions. This armament was insufficient to counter Messerschmitt Bf 109s in daylight.

The first flight by a Hampden was in 1937 and operational aircraft began to arrive at Scampton for No 49 Squadron in No 5 Group during August 1938. In the early part of the war this Group would demonstrate that the type was well suited to minelaying operations.

The distinctive outline of a Hampden bomber in flight.

In 1942 some Hampdens began to serve with Coastal Command for torpedo attacks and some were deployed in Russia for convoy protection work, with the surviving aircraft eventually being handed over to Russian forces.

Bomber Command Hampden sorties ceased in September 1942.

A version of the Hampden with, as they proved, unreliable Napier Dagger engines was produced and was known as the Handley Page Hereford. Herefords briefly reached squadrons, but the type quickly became a trainer. Some were re-engined as Hampdens.

Hampden MK 1 Bomber Command No 5 Group belonging to No 49 Squadron, RAF Scampton, 1940.

Happy Valley – The Ruhr as it was often referred to by Bomber Command aircrew.

Harris, Marshal of the Royal Air Force Sir Arthur Travers Bt (1892-1984) – Born in Cheltenham, at 17 he travelled to Rhodesia, where he undertook a variety of jobs including farming. In October 1914 he joined the 1st Rhodesian Regiment and took part in operations in German South West Africa. He then travelled to Britain and joined the Royal Flying Corps, qualifying as a pilot.

Harris flew against German airships at night, commanded No 38 Squadron and then served in France with Nos 70 and 45 Squadrons. He then commanded No 45 Squadron in England and was awarded the AFC.

In August 1919 Harris received a permanent commission in the RAF as a Squadron Leader. He held a training appointment and became CO of No 31 Squadron in India. After his return to the UK he commanded No 58 Squadron and was appointed OBE in 1927. Attendance at the Army Staff College, Camberley was followed by a staff posting in Egypt and, after an appropriate course, command of the base at Pembroke Dock and No 210 Squadron, operating from there with Supermarine Southampton flying boats.

Though he greatly enjoyed the experience, Wing Commander Harris's sojourn in Wales was short and his career leapt forward with successive appointments at the Air Ministry as Deputy Director of Operations and Plans and Deputy Director Plans.

In 1937, with the rank of Air Commodore, Harris became AOC No 4 Group and, the following year, AOC Palestine and Transjordan.

As an Air Vice-Marshal he commanded No 5 Group and became Deputy Chief of the Air Staff in November 1940, going to Washington DC in 1941 as an acting Air Marshal and Head of British Air Staff.

From February 22 1942 he was Air Officer Commanding in Chief Bomber Command. In fact he had arrived to take command a few days earlier.

Harris discovered many problems including a high level lack of confidence in the ability of the Command to make a major contribution to the war effort and a lack of suitable aircraft. The situation was both illustrated and exacerbated by an ill-judged speech in the House of Commons on February 25 by Sir Stafford Cripps, the Lord Privy Seal, which caused many in Great Britain and the United States to wonder if bombing of Germany was set to become a lower priority.

Harris immediately set about reinvigorating his new command and reassuring doubters on the contribution that the bombers could make.

He was never reluctant to put his position with passion, but historians have often argued that he went too far. A case in point was the transfer of Bomber Command aircraft and crews both to the Middle East and to Coastal Command with, in due course, demands for replacements as well.

Sebastian Cox, in a lecture to the RAF Historical Society in 2009, pointed out the oddity that Dowding of Fighter Command is often praised for his efforts to retain aircraft in 1940, yet Harris is often criticised for taking a similar stance.

"Hence, in June 1942," declared Cox, "Harris addressed a memorandum to the Prime Minister in which he argued that air power had to be concentrated against Germany and not used in 'vastly protracted and avoidable land and sea campaigns'. Not content with that he opined that the diversion of aircraft to Coastal Command meant that the latter was in effect 'merely an obstacle to victory'.

"He did not explain how the population, including his aircrews, were to be fed, or his aircraft fuelled, if the U-boat war was lost. Harris in this instance, as in many others, would have done better to eschew hyperbole, and limit himself to a considered exposition of the impact on his command of such diversions, but that very single-minded-

Air Chief Marshal Harris (second from right) at his High Wycombe HQ.

ness which was to prove such an asset in pulling his command together and focusing it on its task also did not permit him to develop the broadness of vision to see the other side of the coin."

Nonetheless Harris went on to become one of the great, if inevitably controversial, military commanders and one of the most famous war leaders of the 20th century.

His relations with his superiors and colleagues were often difficult, not least with Portal, Chief of the Air Staff, though the two did manage to work together constructively. At least in the earlier parts of his tenure at Bomber Command, Harris had the ear of Churchill and was able to influence him. During the period before and after the D Day landings in 1944 Harris came under the control of General Eisenhower, rather than Portal. That Harris was not always as obstinate and difficult as is sometimes portrayed is illustrated by General Eisenhower's comment that, "Harris actually proved to be one of the most co-operative and effective members of my team; he met every request."

The historian Air Commodore Henry Probert wrote that had the war ended at the time of that comment in September 1944, the verdict on Harris and Bomber Command's contribution might have been much less equivocal than it subsequently became.

That equivocation quickly showed itself – Harris was distressed that no mention of the bomber offensive was made in Churchill's VE Day speech and there was no award of a specific campaign medal to Bomber Command. Harris did not receive the peerage given to other high commanders, though it has emerged that one was available to him. He did become a Marshal of the Royal Air Force, despite never serving as Chief of the Air Staff. In 1953 Churchill, restored as Prime Minister, made an offer of a peerage. Instead Harris took a baronetcy.

Many of the achievements, difficulties and controversies of Harris's time as AOC C-in-C are dealt with in other entries in this book. He was accused of not caring about the fate of those under his command and the nickname of "Butcher" or "Butch" applied to him by his men seems to have owed something both to his perceived determination to kill Germans and his alleged indifference to the RAF casualty rate. He rarely left his HQ at High Wycombe to visit his men and women, yet their rueful regard for him clearly developed into affection as well as respect and he fought their corner in the post-war controversies.

He had other nicknames. To the public he became "Bomber" and to his colleagues he was "Bert", a sobriquet sometimes used in service life for denoting people named Harris.

Arthur Harris had a post-war business career and took up his pen or spoke out when he felt that the wartime deeds of Bomber Command were being misrepresented. As late as 1976 The Guild of Professional Toastmasters named him Best After Dinner Speaker of the Year.

On April 5 1984 Marshal of the Royal Air Force Sir Arthur Harris Bt died at his home in Goring-on-Thames, Berkshire, aged 91.

"The attack on Essen has now inflicted such vast damage that it will in due course take precedence as the greatest victory achieved on any front. You have set a fire in the belly of Germany which will burn the black heart out of Nazidom and whither its grasping limbs at the very roots. Such attacks, which will continue in crescendo, will progressively make it more and more impossible for the enemy to further his aggressions or to hold where he now stands. The great skill and high courage with which you press home to your objectives has already impressed the inevitability of disaster on the whole of Germany and, within the next few months, the hopelessness of their situation will be borne in upon them in a manner which will destroy their capacity for resistance and break their hearts." An example of the morale-boosting messages sent by Harris to his aircrew. This one was distributed in March 1943.

"The proposition of the area offensive was not, of course a purely vengeful or sadistic one. It had its roots in what was practical. If bombers could guarantee to hit no target smaller than a whole city, then a whole city that target must be. And what was practical influenced what seemed strategically desirable. To destroy the will of the German working people, to make them homeless, to make them incapable of performing their manufacturing tasks, this might end the war as effectively as the struggle on the battlefield."

From the obituary of Sir Arthur Harris Bt in The Times, April 7 1984.

High Wycombe – RAF High Wycombe in Buckinghamshire was the headquarters of Bomber Command from 1940 to 1968. Previously the headquarters had been at RAF Uxbridge.

Internment – When RAF aircraft were forced to land in neutral countries, usually as a result of damage or malfunction, the aircraft was normally impounded, with survivors being interned. In other cases evading airmen were arrested, having reached a neutral country. It appears that all airmen held in the Low Countries at the time of the German attack in May 1940 were released. Later a significant number of those interned around Europe, including in Ireland, Spain, Portugal, Sweden and Vichy France, made their way back to the UK with varying degrees of co-operation from the authorities of the country in which they had been held.

An example is the loss of a Halifax II of No 10 Squadron, tasked to attack the German capital ship *Tirpitz* in Fættenfjord, Norway on April 27 1942. The pilot was Wing Commander D C T Bennett (the squadron CO and later Air Officer Commanding in Chief of No 8 Group) and the rest of the crew was Sergeant H Walmsley, Flight Sergeant J Colgan, Sergeant T H A Eyles, Sergeant C R S Forbes, Sergeant J D Murray, RCAF and Flight Lieutenant H G How.

Over the target the aircraft was hit by flak and set on fire and Flight Lieutenant How, the rear gunner, was wounded. After setting course for Sumburgh in Shetland, the pilot realised that this destination could not be achieved and made for Sweden. Eventually the Halifax was abandoned over Norway.

All the crew attempted to reach Sweden, but Eyles, Murray and How were captured by German forces. The others crossed the border into neutral territory, were held by the Swedish authorities, but, over a considerable period, all returned to the UK.

Lack Of Moral Fibre (LMF) – All embracing term for aircrew who directly refused to continue flying or who made it clear by their actions that they were not able or prepared to continue.

Seven decades on, the medical profession has a much better understanding of the causes of such situations and how to treat them. In the inter-war years the bias of medical research in this area had been towards the physical effects of flying, for example lack of oxygen.

Many senior officers were concerned that "LMF" could prove highly infectious and so the tendency was to remove from the station very rapidly anyone considered to be suffering from the condition. In taking this route an airman might save himself from the perils and terrors of further trips over enemy territory, but he would then need a different kind of courage to face humiliation, loss of flying badges and perhaps rank and, more than likely, an allocation to menial duties, or even dismissal from the service.

While the USAAF naturally suffered from the same problem, it appears that its treatment of sufferers was generally less harsh than that meted out by the RAF.

It has been estimated that of all aircrew who served on Bomber Command squadrons and in associated OTUs, 0.4 per cent were classified as suffering from LMF.

"Stress levels for the crews were very high and some did crack under the strain. I was involved in the sequence of events which led to the crew of a Lancaster being deemed to suffer from Lack of Moral Fibre, the dreaded LMF designation. When instructions for a raid were passed to squadron commanders an additional couple of Lancasters were also bombed up in case of any failures in the aircraft designated for that night. One night a crew called in before take-off to report faults in their aircraft. They were directed to one of the reserves which they again reported as faulty. They then found that the third aircraft they were sent to was faulty.

"I had to report the successive failures to the CO. The diagnosis was obvious and swift action followed. The next morning the entire crew had vanished from the station."

Patricia Farquharson recalling her WAAF service with No 75 Squadron at Mepal.

Lancaster Finishing School – Units to which already formed crews were sent to receive the final polish before becoming operational on a squadron.

Leaflet Raids – The dropping of propaganda leaflets by Bomber Command began on the night of September 3/4 1939 and was a particular feature of the early stages of the war.

Officially it was considered that, apart from any influence exerted over German people, such operations were valuable for the experience they gave crews and the information that was obtained on potential targets.

Attention was paid to such matters as wind speed and the heights and distances from targets that led to the most efficient distribution of leaflets.

"It was freezing! The aircraft used to ice up. We had leaflets to drop and if you cut the pack and touched the knife to your skin it would stick. You tried to put as much clothing on as you could because you couldn't get a lot of movement in the aircraft you can't jump up and down to keep warm. One of the things I remember about the winter of 1939/40 was the absolute cold. If I could get a pair of silk stockings I'd wear those, then woollen socks and then flying boots, which were fur-lined, then an inner jacket like a teddy bear with a canvas coating, then a leather jacket with fur, three pairs of gloves – a silk pair, wool and then leather gauntlets. Sheer cold is one of the worst things. You had to sit there and try to think warm."

Greg Gregson, Wireless Operator / Air Gunner. Quoted on the Bomber Command Association website.

Leaving The Aircraft – Considerable thought was given by officialdom and by individual crew members on the best ways of leaving different aircraft in an emergency.

For example, on the Halifax the forward escape hatch was under the navigator's chair which folded back against the bulkhead . The Navigator/Wireless Operator and Bomb Aimer would normally leave through that hatch. There were two escape hatches in the roof which would be used by the Mid Upper Gunner and the Flight Engineer. The Pilot would exit by the canopy and the Rear Gunner would rotate his turret to athwartship and fall out backwards. Naturally, improvisation was sometimes required.

Light Night Striking Force – Developed within the Pathfinder Force, the LNSF used Mosquitos, often in fast "nuisance" attacks with 4,000lb High Capacity bombs ("cookies") against German industry.

Lincoln Cathedral – The twin towers of the cathedral on a hill standing out from the flatness around were a great landmark for airborne navigators and airmen often visited the cathedral and its grounds where the WVS would dispense refreshments.

An early postcard view showing the distinctive twin towers of Lincoln Cathedral.

In 2006 a ledger stone was placed in the Cathedral at the entrance to the Airmen's Chapel, facing the Bomber Command window and to the right of the Book of Remembrance that contains the names of more than 27,000 aircrew who were killed when flying from Lincolnshire airbases.

The inscription on the stone reads, "Dedicated to the men and women of Bomber Command, 1939-1945, over 50,000 of whom gave their lives in defence of our liberty." The unveiling ceremony was performed by wartime veterans.

The cathedral's West Front includes part of the original building from 1072, though much of what can be seen today dates from the 13th century.

A copy of the Magna Carta is kept in the library as well as the Lincoln Chapter Bible (c1100) and a school book from 1410 containing the first known rhyme about Robin Hood.

Traditional skills are preserved through a team of 30 men and women, including stonemasons, glaziers, carpenters, plumbers, conservators and archivists.

Another Lincolnshire landmark, extremely helpful to inexperienced navigators, was "Boston Stump", the church of St Botolph's in the Lincolnshire town, with its spectacular tower. Work on the present building began in 1309. The tower is a 15th and 16th century creation.

Lindemann, Frederick – see Lord Cherwell

Lockheed Ventura – Designed by Lockheed as a more advanced version of the Hudson, with parentage that also owed much to the Lodestar passenger aircraft.

The first flight was in July 1941 and the first operational examples for Bomber Command reached No 21 Squadron at Methwold in November 1942. A bomb load of up to 2,500lb could be carried and there was normally a crew of four. The Ventura proved as vulnerable as other RAF types in unescorted daylight operations. Overall its contribution to Bomber Command was not significant and aircraft were eventually transferred to Coastal Command.

The type is best remembered for the attack on an Amsterdam power station on May 3 1943, which resulted in both heavy casualties and a Victoria Cross for Squadron Leader Leonard Trent, the leader of the formation. Trent became a PoW and his award was not gazetted until March 1 1946.

With the name Harpoon, the PV2 version could be found in the Pacific theatre serving a patrol bomber with the United States Navy in 1944 and 1945.

Ludlow-Hewitt, Air Chief Marshal Sir Edgar Rainey (1886-1973) – The son of a clergyman, he was commissioned in the Royal Irish Rifles in 1905. He learned to fly in 1914 and, at the beginning of the Great War, he became a probationary member of the Royal Flying Corps. Considered an outstanding pilot, he was awarded the MC in 1916, the DSO two years later and was six times mentioned in despatches during the war. He commanded No 3 Squadron and a Wing.

Between the wars Ludlow-Hewitt was Commandant of the RAF Staff College, Andover, Air Officer Commanding Iraq, Director of Operations and Intelligence at the Air Ministry and Air Officer Commanding in India.

From 1937 he was Air Officer Commanding in Chief, Bomber Command. He was a disciple of the theory propounded by Viscount Trenchard that future wars would be won by the power of bombing, but had to accept that the RAF bomber force was small and that little thought had been given to such matters as finding targets. In addition, Fighter Command was the beneficiary of most of the scientific development work available to the RAF as war approached.

Ludlow-Hewitt had considerable intellect, but was not tough enough to deal with the situation in which he found himself. He left Bomber Command in April 1940 and for five years served in a role that suited his talents – RAF Inspector-General.

MacRobert's Reply – The name applied to a number of RAF aircraft, the first of which was a Short Stirling that entered service in 1941.

This event followed the donation of £25,000 from Lady MacRobert, the Massachusetts born widow of Sir Alexander MacRobert, first Baronet, who had died in 1922. In turn each of their three sons succeeded to the Baronetcy and each was killed serving with the RAF, Sir Alisdair in 1938, Sir Roderic in 1941 and Sir Iain also in 1941.

Lady MacRobert's letter to the Air Minister enclosing the cheque described her gesture as "a mother's immediate reply" and included the words, "I have no more sons to wear the MacRobert badge or carry it in the fight —— but if I had 10 sons I know they would all have followed that line of duty."

Lady MacRobert attended the ceremony when the original MacRobert's Reply, Stirling N8086 entered RAF service with No 15 Squadron, carrying the family coat of arms on its nose.

This aircraft was lost in an accident in February 1942 and was replaced as MacRobert's Reply by Stirling W7531. This second aircraft was shot down on a gardening trip to the Danish coast on the night of May 17/18 1942. It was carrying a crew of nine (including one officer along for the ride) and there was one survivor who became a PoW.

The MacRobert's Reply name was next carried on Hurricanes.

Mailly-le-Camp – In the run-up to D Day, an attack on Panzer barracks east of Paris on the moonlit night of May 3/4

1944. There was also a small operation against Montdidier airfield. Both targets should have been "easy" according to the thinking of the time and aircrew were only able to add one third to the total of operations counting towards their tours.

However, major breakdowns in communications occurred over Mailly-le-Camp, leading to many aircraft not receiving the order to bomb. The use of a datum point, marked by yellow target indicators, proved a considerable aid to German night fighters. The extent of the communications problem was illustrated by crews reporting hearing over radios, as they tried to take instructions from the master bomber, an American station, which at one point played *Deep in the Heart of Texas*.

A memory for survivors is the profusion of bombers they saw going down, sometimes several at once. The number of aircraft involved in the operation and lost by Bomber Command was 49, mostly Lancasters. Nonetheless considerable damage and German casualties on the ground were achieved.

"More than 300 airmen failed to return that night, of whom 258 were killed; most of those killed are buried in the cemeteries of villages surrounding Mailly-le-Camp.

"Recognising that they lost their lives in the fight for the freedom we all enjoy today, these communities honour the dead airmen and care for their graves as if they were their own sons.

"On each anniversary of the raid the local citizens including many school children and young people, the French Army, and representatives of the Resistance – many of whom assisted RAF evaders – attend a series of services organised by the French L'Association Mailly 3/4 Mai 1944, which culminates in a military parade on the French Army base at the memorial erected by L'Association Mailly.

"British and Commonwealth veterans, relatives of the fallen and other supporters are made very welcome and seek to participate in these events to honour, not only the aircrew and French people who died in the raid, but also the gallant French Resistants who risked – and in some cases lost – their lives helping survivors who came down in France."

From the website of the Mailly-le-Camp Commemoration Support Group.

Main Force – Term applied to the majority of squadrons whose principal task was straightforward bombing, rather than marking, jamming and other duties.

Manna (Operation) – In the closing days of the war in Europe Bomber Command dropped supplies for civilians over the part of The Netherlands still at least nominally under German control. This was done with the consent of the German authorities.

The USAAF version of Manna was Operation Chowhound.

When veterans visited the memorial in 2010 Jack Cook, 84, who was a wireless operator on No 100 Squadron, was quoted by the *Sunday Times* as saying:- "The people were on tops of houses waving sheets, towels, anything white. They still treat us like heroes. We're not. We were just doing our job."

Master Bomber – Highly experienced pilot appointed to direct the bombing of a target.

Master Of Ceremonies – A less formal name for the Master Bomber on a raid.

Memorial – In early 2011 plans for a Bomber Command Memorial were at last close to fruition. Planning consent had been received for a site on the edge of Green Park, close to the

RAF Club and Hyde Park Corner. An imposing and traditional design had been created by Liam O'Connor, architect responsible for the Armed Services Memorial at Cannock, Staffordshire, remembering servicemen and women who have lost their lives since the end of the Second World War. The sculptor appointed was Philip Jackson, whose works include the equestrian sculpture of The Queen in Windsor Great Park.

Fundraising was being energetically undertaken.

"(the casualty figures) are so appalling that we risk becoming inured to what they truly mean. Behind each death was a family – parents, friends, often a wife and children, and each would have been utterly devastated by the loss of its loved one – as those who survive no doubt remain so today. For someone of my generation, the scale of this loss is almost impossible to comprehend. Yet comprehend it we must. Each one of those young men died for you and for me.

"So much of the analysis of Bomber Command's role in the Second World War has been mired in controversy that it is sometimes forgotten what these young men went through for us. Their average age was only 22. They were all volunteers. They set forth into the unknown by day and by night, often in freezing conditions. Over enemy territory, they were under near constant attack. And they did this night after night – for up to 12 hours at a time. Just try to imagine that – imagine finding the courage to overcome your fear to climb into your flying gear again, and again, knowing what will confront you. As a flyer myself, I find this quite extraordinary. But they did it – tens of thousands of times.

"A memorial to the crews of Bomber Command has been half a century too long in coming.

"Having seen the plans for this sublimely beautiful memorial, I do feel that at last their wait is at an end. This will be a truly fitting epitaph to the other – sometimes forgotten – Second World War heroes of the Royal Air Force. A yew tree, a gift from the German nation, is to be planted in the Garden of Remembrance nearby. There can be no greater message of reconciliation than this.

"Today, only some 3000 men of Bomber Command remain with us. It is vital, therefore, that this memorial be erected now, while they are still alive and able to appreciate our Nation's gratitude to them, and to their fallen comrades. My great-grandmother, Queen Elizabeth The Queen Mother, was a great champion of Bomber Command. Instinctively, she knew that it was right to honour these young men and their extraordinary sacrifice. As with so much else in her life, her instincts were correct.

You might ask, with a champion such as Queen Elizabeth, what need is there for me to ask you to support this appeal. All I can say is that, as the Patron of the Battle of Britain Memorial Flight – with its magnificent guardian of these memories, the lone Lancaster, 'The City of Lincoln' – my own realisation of what these men undertook has only recently really dawned on me – as I think it has with many of my generation in other ways.

"Mine is but one amongst many voices, urging all those who value the freedoms we enjoy today to contribute whatever you feel you can towards the creation of this wonderful monument. And for those who have already supported the appeal it is not for me to say thank you, but I can only imagine the gratitude of the veterans of Bomber Command, their families and the Royal Air Force."

Prince William of Wales, as Patron of the Battle of Britain Memorial Flight, writing in November 2010 in support of the Bomber Command Memorial.

Navigator – One navigator, veteran of more than 70 operations, summarised the role as, "The Navigator had to know his position at any time by dead reckoning from his last known position (pinpoint from a sighted position on the ground, radar or astro fix) had to calculate wind speed and direction from the foregoing and recalculate courses and ETA to destination."

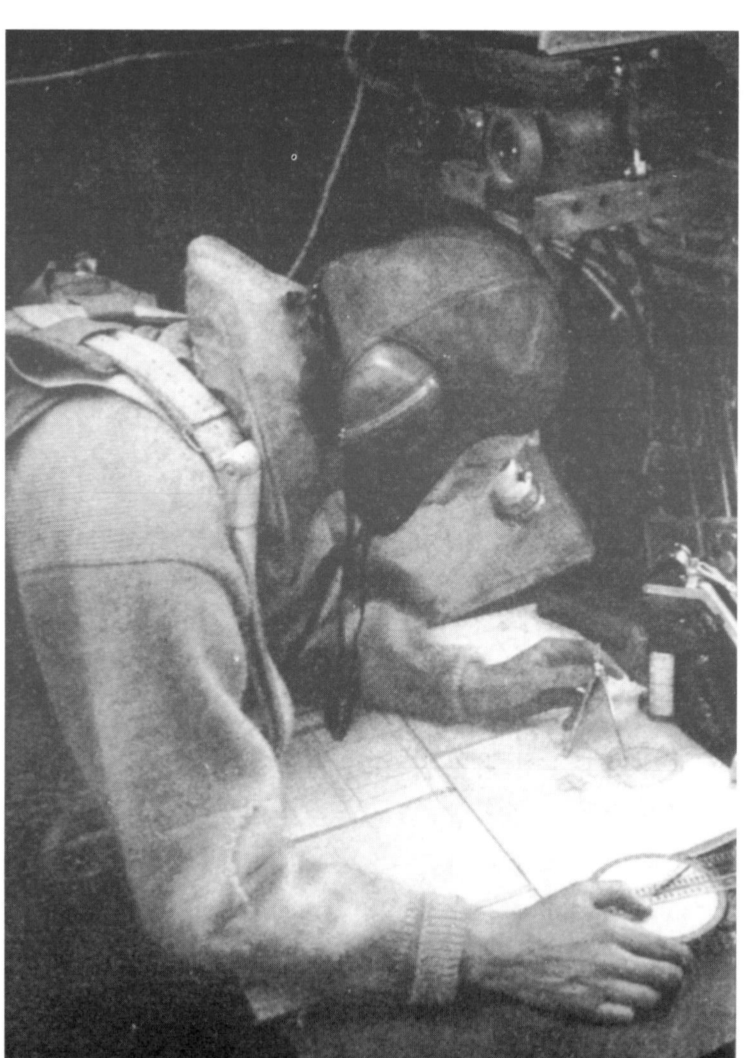

A Bomber Command navigator at work in the early days of the war.

He was too modest to point out that the navigator played such a major role that there were frequent occasions when the pilot (and the rest of the crew) had to put total trust in the Navigator's judgement.

Many Navigators had begun their training with the intention of becoming pilots, failed or otherwise left the pilots' course and re-mustered.

"Fly north with a dash of west while I sort myself out," alleged remark by Tommy Broom after the Mosquito flown by Ivor Broom had sought to escape from being coned for 15 minutes over Berlin.

Early in the war the official name for the role was Observer.

Newall, Sir Cyril Louis Norton (1886-1963) – Born in India, attended RMA Sandhurst and was commissioned (in 1905) into the Royal Warwickshire Regiment.

Air Chief Marshal Sir Cyril Newall, Chief of the Air Staff at the outbreak of war.

Newall served on the North West Frontier and, in 1911, transferred to the 2nd Gurkha Rifles. Having learnt to fly in 1911, he gained his RFC wings in 1913. Initially an instructor, he was promoted to Major in 1915 and, later in the year, took command of No 12 Squadron, leading it in France.

On January 3 1916, Newall led three Corporals into a burning shed containing many bombs and played a key role in removing bombs and extinguishing the fire. He received the Albert Medal. After his death living holders of the award were offered the opportunity to exchange it for the George Cross.

After the war Newall was granted a permanent commission in the RAF. He commanded the school of technical training for apprentices at Halton and served at the Air Ministry. As an Air Vice-Marshal in the early thirties he was head of RAF Middle East based in Cairo. He was then Air Member for Supply and Organisation. In 1935 he became KCB and was promoted to Air Marshal.

In September 1937 Air Chief Marshal Newall took up the post of Chief of the Air Staff. He was determined to make the RAF ready for war and believed that Britain could best be defended by having a powerful bomber force for counter offence.

However, Sir Thomas Inskip, Minister for Co-ordination of Defence, espoused the theory that the priority was a strong fighter force capable of resisting German bombers. Newall was supported by Viscount Swinton, Secretary of State for Air, in his opposition to Inskip, but the latter won the argument in Cabinet. Newall's consolation was that he managed to gain authorisation for higher expenditure, which ensured that the work of making the RAF ready for war in the short term could move forward alongside long term expansion plans.

Newall regarded the Munich agreement of 1938 as a national humiliation and re-doubled his efforts to make ready for conflict.

When war came he was forced to commit bombers, fighters and army co-operation units to operations across the Channel, against his own judgement. He resisted pressure from the other services to bomb Germany, following the invasion of Norway, but changed his position as the Blitzkreig began, proposing successfully that attacks on the Ruhr should begin.

During 1940 Newall lost influential supporters and suffered from a "whispering campaign" suggesting that he was not up to the job.

As the year moved on he gave some the impression that he was tired and not in control of events.

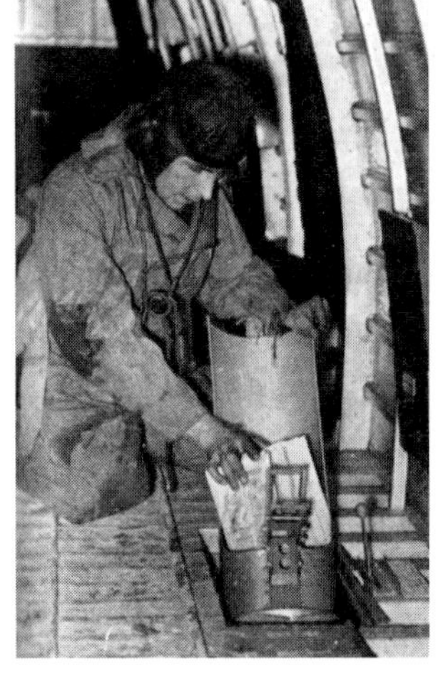

Leaflets being discharged through the aircraft's flare chute.

Promotion to Marshal of the Royal Air Force and admission to the Order of Merit followed and he became Governor-General of New Zealand in 1941, serving until 1946. He became a Baron in 1946.

Newall disliked contact with journalists and did not write memoirs. His contribution to preparing the RAF for war has, partly for those reasons, rarely been highlighted.

To Marshal of the Royal Air Force Sir John Slessor (Chief of the Air Staff 1950-52), Newall was, "the prime architect of the wartime air force".

Nickel – The term for leaflet dropping operations.

A flight of North American Mitchells being prepared for take off.

North American B-25 Mitchell – A medium bomber particularly associated with No 2 Group in Bomber Command. It was named after the American aviation pioneer, Colonel "Billy" Mitchell. The first flight was on August 19 1940. The type came to be regarded as reliable and robust.

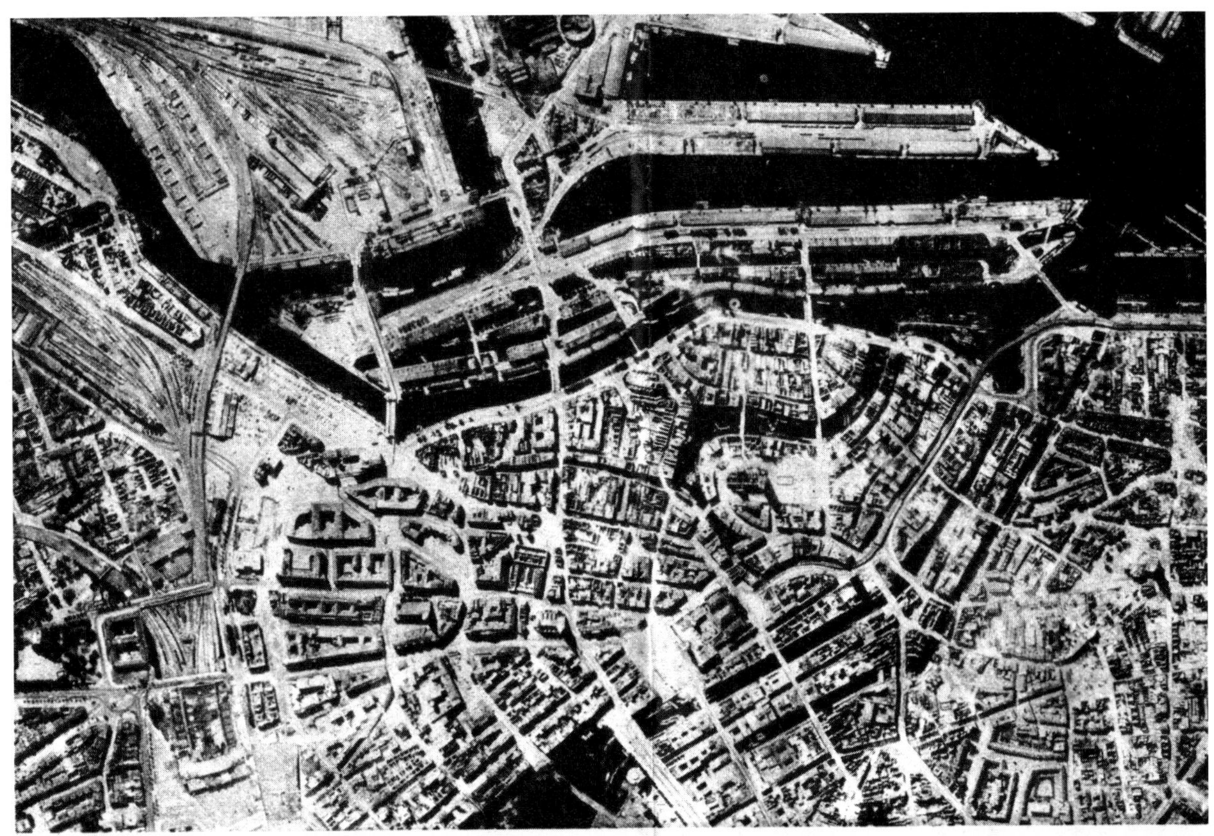

DAS WAR HAMBURG

Teil einer Luftaufnahme nach den Angriffen der RAF Der rotumrandete Bildausschnitt ist umseitig in Vergrösserung wiedergegeben.

"This was Hamburg" is the message to German people who read this leaflet dropped on them by Bomber Command. It comes from the collection of Peter Piper a rear gunner with No 7 Squadron who retained one example of each leaflet he handled.

Fame came to the Mitchell in April 1942 when aircraft took off from the *USS Hornet* to attack Tokyo.

Nose Art – Bomber Command aircraft sometimes carried nose art, though the practice was less widespread than it was amongst US bombers. A favourite for the RAF was Jane, the Daily Mirror cartoon character. Witches were another favoured subject.

At the Yorkshire Air Museum, Elvington, there is a reconstruction of a Halifax, using part of the fuselage of an aircraft that forced-landed on the Isle of Lewis in 1945, as well as parts from other aircraft. This reconstruction is named "Friday the 13th", honouring Halifax LV907 which carried that name and flew 128 operations with No 158 Squadron. Elvington was a wartime Bomber Command airfield.

Phantom of the Ruhr – an especially famous Lancaster

The crew of a Lancaster pose beside their aircraft at Kirmington in June 1944. The nose art represents "Tiki", a Maori good luck charm chosen by the pilot John Boles, a New Zealander.

A well known Lancaster was EE139 of Nos 100 and 550 Squadrons, given the name, "Phantom of the Ruhr" by its first crew, with the nose art devised by the Flight Engineer, "Ben" Bennett. The Phantom achieved 121 operations. In the spring of 2011, the Lancaster in the collection of the Battle of Britain Memorial Flight was carrying the "Phantom of the Ruhr" name.

"God Bless Our Ship", "Flak Ducker", "Lili Marlene", "Ark Angel", "Linda Lou", "Windy Winnie" and "Miss Fortune" were examples of names applied to USAAF bombers – often, of course, the names were accompanied by paintings of

The nose art on this Lancaster of No 463 Squadron RAAF, at RAF Waddington, is of a cow with the title "Whoa Bessie".

young ladies dressed in less than was normally considered orthodox.

Sometimes wives, fiancées and girl friends would be honoured. A case in point was the USAAF Liberator, *Ruth-Less,* named by the pilot Frank Slough after his wife. Flown by another pilot the aircraft took off from Shipdham on February 2 1944 bound for the Vl site at Watten between

Bomber Command veterans visit the Battle of Britain Memorial Flight Lancaster at Jersey Airport in 2010.

Calais and St Omer in France. The Liberator aborted and then crashed on the Downs near Eastbourne.

Since 1995 a memorial has marked the spot, giving the names of the eight men who died instantly and the remaining two crew members who succumbed to their injuries. The memorial includes the words:-

In memory of the crew of a B-24D Liberator Bomber

No. 41-24282 BAR Y ''RUTH-LESS''

of

506 Squadron, 44th Bombardment Group, 8th. U.S.A.A.F.

Who all lost their lives, when,

badly damaged by enemy action and in very low cloud,

the aircraft crashed here on February 2nd. 1944.

OUR FRIENDS AND ALLIES

FAR FROM HOME

See also entry for MacRobert's reply.

Nuisance Raids – Raids carried out with the prime purpose of preventing workers in factories supplying the enemy having a good night's sleep.

Nuremberg – Bavarian city targeted by Bomber Command. The operation on March 30/31 1944 has gone down as one of the Command's disasters. Weather forecasts made the decision to attack marginal and the wind was not as forecast during the outward flight, taking many of the almost 800 Lancasters and Halifaxs off course. Relatively little damage was caused in the target area and many aircraft bombed the wrong place, including Schweinfurt more than 50 miles from Nuremberg.

The Bomber Command loss rate for the night was a very high 11.6 per cent.

Oboe – Blind-bombing system using two ground stations and a pulse repeater in the aircraft. Oboe was highly accurate and not susceptible to jamming, but had a limited range and capacity. Oboe was used to effect by the Mosquitos of No 109 Squadron in the Pathfinder Force.

Observer – See entry for Navigator.

Oil – The extent to which attacks on oil installations serving the enemy might have hastened the end of the war has gone down as one of the great controversies of the bomber offensive.

Critics of Air Chief Marshal Harris have accused him of disobeying orders in late 1944 to attack oil targets, though in fact no such specific order was ever given.

Bomb damage at a benzine plant in the Ruhr.

Harris did not attach the great importance to oil as a target that Portal for one did, as he made clear to the Chief of the Air Staff, nevertheless a post war study of oil as a factor in the German war effort produced by the British Chiefs of Staff concluded that in the three months, October, November, December 1944, there were only seven nights and three days when weather allowed oil installations to be treated as a target and they were not.

Sebastian Cox, head of the RAF Air Historical Branch, in a paper to the RAF Historical Society in 2009, also drew attention to the problems of defining types of targets for the purpose of producing comparative figures.

He pointed out that, for instance, experts at the time considered that most of Germany's oil production in September 1944 came from benzol plants which produced oil as a by-product of coke ovens. As a result of this they were largely to be found in the Ruhr, an area frequently the subject of Bomber Command area attacks.

Sebastian Cox also noted that, "According to the American official history, not by and large notable for its sympathetic view of Harris, by the end of November 1944 'all of the RAF's synthetic oil targets were suspended because they were no longer operating'! That statement alone seems to me to cast a great deal of doubt on some of the criticisms (of lack of attacks on oil targets)."

Old Lags – Name by which Sir Arthur Harris referred, in the post war era, to the aircrew who had served under him. The sobriquet was enthusiastically taken up by many of the men themselves.

Operational Training Unit – For many Bomber Command aircrew the OTU provided the final training before they arrived on a squadron.

Panacea Targets – A dismissive term used by Air Chief Marshal Harris, usually indicating targets proposed by those outside his command (for example the Air Ministry and the Ministry of Economic Warfare) with the objective of doing major damage to a specific contributor to the German war effort. Examples were oil and rubber installations.

Pathfinder Force (PFF) – An elite force of target marking crews formed on August 15 1942 with its headquarters at Wyton, Huntingdonshire. Air Vice-Marshal D C T Bennett became its commander and it would become No 8 Group within Bomber Command. Later the headquarters would be at Castle Hill House, Huntingdon.

Air Vice-Marshal Donald "Pathfinder" Bennett.

Donald Bennett was an Australian who had served in that country's air force before joining the RAF in 1931. He later worked for Imperial Airways, became Flight Superintendent of the Atlantic Ferry Service and rejoined the RAF in 1941.

The formation of the PFF, of which Lord Cherwell was a proponent, had been opposed by Sir Arthur Harris, particularly on the grounds that it would be difficult to form a Group with elite crews and there would be a negative impact on morale in the other Groups.

Harris lost the debate, in part because of the reasoned arguments put forward by Group Captain S O Bufton of the Directorate of Bomber Operations at the Air Ministry. Bufton based his analysis to some extent on comments by his

Calais is the target photographed from a PFF aircraft in September 1944.

contacts in Bomber Command obtained behind the back of the Air Officer Commanding in Chief.

The controversy never went away and stirred again in the spring of 1944 when Harris gave No 5 Group enhanced status and transferred to it three PFF squadrons.

The PFF used Lancasters and Mosquitos and a wide variety of target marking devices. Possibly its greatest success was the overcoming of the industrial haze over targets during the Battle of the Ruhr.

"An indication of the terrible power – according to the standards of that time – possessed by this force can be seen from the result of the raid on July 25/26 1943. On that night more than 600 bombers delivered a fierce 50-minute assault on Essen, home of the huge Krupps armament works. They bombed on accurately-placed ground markers dropped by nine Oboe-equipped PFF Mosquitoes and inflicted more damage on Essen than all the previous attacks put together. Hitler's Propaganda Minister, Dr Goebbels, recorded in his diary for July 28: 'The last raid on Essen caused a complete stoppage of production in the Krupps works. Speer is much concerned and worried.' On the morning after the raid Dr Gustav Krupp von Bohlen und Halbach came down to his office, took one look at the blazing remnants of his works and fell down in a fit." RAF website.

"I do not think the formation of a first XV at rugby makes little boys play any less enthusiastically." The scientist Sir Henry Tizard commenting on objections to the PFF.

Those who served with the PFF received promotion, increased pay and could earn the PFF badge. They also flew tours of 45 operations. There were many acts of great heroism among the PFF crews, but Air Vice-Marshal Bennett stuck to his dictat that no living member of the force would wear the ribbon of the VC.

Peenemunde – Attack on the night of August 17/18 1943 on the Peenemunde complex on the Baltic coast of Germany where development work was being carried on relating to both the V-1 flying bomb and the V-2 rocket, both of which would be launched against England.

Almost 600 heavy bombers took part in the operation, under the direction of the Master Bomber, Group Captain John Searby, CO of No 83 Squadron in No 8 Group, a man seen as exemplifying the qualities of calmness and soundness required for the task, as well as having the necessary experience.

The attack inflicted considerable damage, though bombs began falling on a nearby camp for foreign labourers, a mistake corrected by Searby. Unusually the targets specified included the living and sleeping area, with the intention of killing or incapacitating as many scientific and technical staff as possible.

However, 40 bombers were lost on a cloudless and moonlit night, with 288 Bomber Command aircrew being killed or taken prisoner.

"The target looked as though one wave of bombers had already hit it and that the whole country was erupting into something terrible. The explosions below were so tremendous that, as we made our pass over the area, it was like riding a car over a ploughed field. There was a great sigh of relief when we altered course for home and my poor old backside muscles relaxed a bit. They had been going 'threepenny bit and two and six' for at least half an hour and it felt good to be on the way home knowing that this target had been completely destroyed." Sergeant A C Farmer, No 12 Squadron, quoted in The Peenemunde Raid by Martin Middlebrook.

Air Marshal Sir Richard Peirse.

Peirse, Air Chief Marshal Sir Richard Edmund Charles (1892-1970) – Learned to fly at Brooklands and was commissioned in the Royal Naval Reserve. He served on the Western Front and was awarded the DSO. In 1919 he received a permanent commission in the RAF as a Squadron Leader.

In 1937 Peirse became Director of Operations and Intelligence and Deputy Chief of the Air Staff. He became an additional member of the Air Council in October 1939 and Vice Chief of the Air Staff, under Air Chief Marshal Sir Cyril Newall, in April 1940. When Newall was replaced as CAS by Portal, Peirse became Air Officer Commanding in Chief, Bomber Command, taking up the post on October 25 1940.

Peirse remained in the post until January 1942 when he was sent to the Far East on being replaced by Sir Arthur Harris. He oversaw a period when Bomber Command was beginning to go on the offensive, despite suffering from a lack of suitable aircraft. Even allowing for the problems he encountered, confidence in his decisions amongst senior figures waned during 1941.

In August 1942 Peirse was promoted to Air Chief Marshal and from November 1943 he commanded all Allied air forces in south east Asia, enjoying an excellent relationship with his superior Lord Louis Mountbatten. The relationship came under strain, however, with increasing evidence that a relationship existed between Peirse and Lady Auchinleck. Eventually it was announced that Peirse would be replaced by Air Chief Marshal Sir Trafford Leigh-Mallory, but Leigh-Mallory died in an air crash on the way out to take up his new appointment. Nonetheless Peirse left his new command in November 1944 and the RAF in May 1945. He married Lady Auchinleck after both had obtained divorces.

Pierson, Reginald Kirshaw (1891-1948) – "Rex" Pierson was born in Norfolk, where his father was rector of Little Fransham near East Dereham. The young Pierson joined Vickers as an apprentice in 1908. He learned to fly at Brooklands and became Chief Technician of Vickers in 1914. During the First World War he was responsible for the design of the Vimy bomber, which also became well known for its long distance flights.

For many years Pierson was Vickers Chief Designer, overseeing the design of all the well known types of the era including the Wellesley and the Wellington. In 1945 he became Chief Engineer of the Vickers-Armstrong group, with George (later Sir George) Edwards succeeding him in the design post. Pierson was taken ill with cancer in 1947 and died early the following year.

In 1952 the Royal Aeronautical Society launched the R K Pierson Memorial Lecture which continues to this day. It was the first of the Society's lectures to be named in honour of an individual.

"Mr R K Pierson – designer of the Wellington". Heading for obituary in *The Times*, January 12 1948.

Pilot – In the Royal Air Force, unlike the Luftwaffe, the pilot was always considered to be in command of the aircraft. This applied even if other members of the crew held higher rank.

Decision making for pilots as illustrated in a letter from Squadron Leader James Sindall to his wife. He had flown a Wellington of No 115 Squadron.

Royal Air Force,

MARHAM, KING'S LYNN,

Norfolk

12.7.41

The time is 5.30 and I have just come back from Abingdon where I went with Doc Maley (sic) to see one of my crew in hospital where he is with a broken leg. I had just read your letter, in which you ask me if I had a good party that night. We ***did!*** We went to Osnabruck and came back to find everywhere covered with cloud at ground level. We arrived back over the aerodrome at 3.30 in the morning and were told to go to Abingdon where it was clear and we could get down.

At 4.15 we were very short of petrol so I tried the first of the distress calls. But there was such a row going on in the air, everybody calling for help (!!!), that I could get no result. So eventually I sent out S.O.S. We got an answer from Hull (they listen in for S.O.S's) who said go to Abingdon. They then telephoned Abingdon which took 20 minutes or so to say let these people in at once.

Well, we contacted Abingdon as soon as Hull told us to go there, but as they did not know by then that we were in an S.O.S they just decided to let us take our turn with the other machines.

At about 4.30 the engines cut and I pushed the crew out. I decided to stay on for a moment or two to let all the petrol burn up so that she would not burn when she crashed. Then a funny thing happened. They picked up again and spluttered and banged and I was able to fly for another hour! It was due to the change in altitude and weight with the crew gone.

The letter sent by J H Sindall. Courtesy Squadron Leader Tim Sindall.

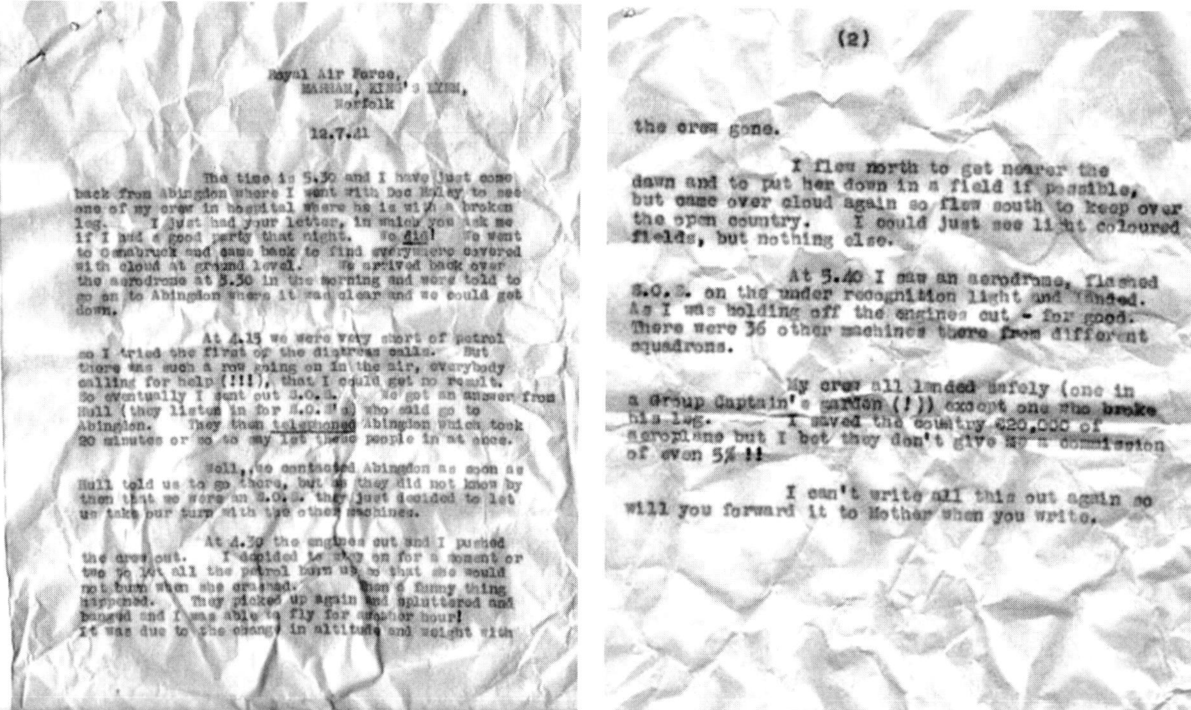

Royal Air Force,
MARHAM, KING'S LYNN,
Norfolk

12.7.41

The time is 5.30 and I have just come back from Abingdon where I went with Doc [illegible] to see one of my crew in hospital where he is with a broken leg. I just had your letter, in which you ask me if I had a good party that night. We did! We went to Osnabruck and came back to find everywhere covered with cloud at ground level. We arrived back over the aerodrome at 3.30 in the morning and were told to go on to Abingdon where it was clear and we could get down.

At 4.15 we were very short of petrol so I tried the first of the distress calls. But there was such a row going on in the air, everybody calling for help (!!!), that I could get no result. So eventually I sent out S.O.S. We got an answer from Hull (they listen in for S.O.S's) who said go to Abingdon. They then telephoned Abingdon which took 20 minutes or so to say let these people in at once.

Well, we contacted Abingdon as soon as Hull told us to go there, but as they did not know by then that we were an S.O.S. they just decided to let us take our turn with the other machines.

At 4.30 the engines cut and I pushed the crew out. I decided to stay on for a moment or two to let all the petrol burn up so that she would not burn when she crashed. Then a funny thing happened. They picked up again and spluttered and banged and I was able to fly for another hour! It was due to the change in altitude and weight with

(2)

the crew gone.

I flew north to get nearer the dawn and to put her down in a field if possible, but came over cloud again so flew south to keep over the open country. I could just see light coloured fields, but nothing else.

At 5.40 I saw an aerodrome, flashed S.O.S. on the under recognition light and landed. As I was holding off the engines cut - for good. There were 36 other machines there from different squadrons.

My crew all landed safely (one in a Group Captain's garden (!)) except one who broke his leg. I saved the country £20,000 of aeroplane but I bet they don't give me a commission of even 5% !!

I can't write all this out again so will you forward it to Mother when you write.

I flew north to get nearer the dawn and to put her down in a field if possible, but came over cloud again so flew south to keep over open country. I could just see light coloured fields, but nothing else.

At 5.40 I saw an aerodrome, flashed S.O.S. on the under recognition light and landed. As I was holding off the engines cut – for good. There were 36 other machines there from different squadrons.

My crew all landed safely (one in a Group Captain's garden (!)) except one who broke his leg. I saved the country £20,000 of an aeroplane but I bet they don't give me a commission of even 5%!!

I can't write all this out again so will you forward it to Mother when you write.

Portal, Marshal of the Royal Air Force Viscount Portal of Hungerford – Charles Frederick Algernon Portal was born on May 21 1893 of Huguenot descent. He was usually known as "Peter" both in his family and, later, amongst service and other friends.

A career in the law was what he intended, but within days of the outbreak of The Great War he had volunteered to serve as a dispatch rider in the Royal Engineers. Within a few more days he was in France with the British Expeditionary Force, receiving a commission on September 26. A request for attachment to the Royal Flying Corps was granted and Portal joined No 3 Squadron as an air observer in July 1915. The next month he was seriously injured in a motor cycle accident while on leave, but quickly returned to France.

Portal qualified as a pilot, served in No 60 Squadron and returned to No 3 Squadron as a Flight Commander, flying reconnaissance and artillery observation sorties. An immediate MC was gazetted at the beginning of 1917, marking his "conspicuous skill and gallantry" during the Somme offensive. He would later also receive the DSO.

Command of No 16 Squadron, when Portal was a temporary Major, followed. A bar to the DSO was awarded for his leadership of the squadron in support of Canadian troops during the German spring offensive in 1918.

With a post-war permanent commission, Squadron Leader Portal was chief flying instructor at the RAF College, Cranwell and was on the first course at the RAF Staff College, Andover. He served at the Air Ministry and attended the senior officers' war course at the Royal Naval College, Greenwich.

Portal took command of No 7 Squadron in 1927. Flying from Worthy Down, in Vickers Virginias, the squadron became recognised for outstanding bombing accuracy.

Time at the Imperial Defence College followed before he became Deputy Director of Plans on the Air Staff. In 1934 he took command of British forces in Aden and enhanced his reputation by the way he restored order after aggression by Quteibi tribesmen. Promotion to Air Commodore came at the beginning of 1935.

After a spell on the directing staff at the Imperial Defence College Portal found himself at the Air Ministry and at the heart of the expansion of the RAF to meet the perceived threat from Germany. As Director of Organisation, key tasks involved the development of specialist units for operational flying training and the creation of more airfields.

On February 1 1939 Portal joined the Air Staff as Air Member for Personnel. On April 4 1940 he became Air Officer Commanding in Chief, Bomber Command and held this post until his translation to Chief of the Air Staff in late October that year. In July 1940 he had become KCB and was therefore known as Air Marshal Sir Charles Portal from that time.

In his book, *High Commanders of the RAF*, Air Commodore Henry Probert quoted a number of descriptions of Portal by those who were close to him or had studied him. Words and phrases deployed included, "took some knowing, often appearing cold, remote and enigmatic" (John Terraine), "those close to him often saw the kind and human side" Probert himself, "highly supportive and had tremendous authority" (R V Jones), "wise and very patient" (Sir John Slessor), "complete professional" (Maurice Dean), "the real brains in the Chiefs of Staff" (Lord Tedder), "great co-operator" (Earl Mountbatten).

Prisoners of War – Almost 10,000 Bomber Command aircrew became prisoners of war. Many were treated in accordance with the Geneva Convention, though there were plenty of examples of this not being the case. The Geneva Convention was most notoriously flouted when 50 recaptured prisoners, including Bomber Command men, were murdered after the "Great Escape" from Stalag Luft lll in March 1944.

For some incarceration would last almost six years. In the opening hours of the war a number of Bomber Command aircraft did not return from various operations. Amongst the crews of those aircraft there were fatalities and two men became prisoners of the Germans.

These two were Sergeant George Booth (observer) and AC1 Larry Slattery (Wireless Operator/Air Gunner) of Blenheim N6240 of No 107 Squadron based at Wattisham. Sent to attack shipping at Wilhelmshaven, the aircraft was shot down in the target area and the pilot, Sergeant A S Prince was killed.

The Germans initially gave Booth and Slattery excellent treatment, apparently regarding them as useful pawns in the propaganda war. Things changed for Slattery, discovered by his captors to be a skilled violinist, when he declined their suggestions that he should perform and also take part in intelligence work, in exchange for eventual repatriation.

During their long captivity Booth and Slattery were both promoted to Warrant Officer.

An unorthodox way to be taken prisoner was experienced by some of the crew of Lancaster 1 W4107 of No 49 Squadron based at Scampton. On the night of November 22/23 1942 the target for Flight Sergeant Eric Singleton and his crew was Stuttgart. After releasing its load the aircraft was hit by flak, causing leaks to fuel tanks and a fire in the starboard inner engine; then a flare was accidentally ignited.

The pilot ordered the crew to bale out but decided to see for how long he could continue flying. Four of the crew left the aircraft, but the mid upper gunner, Sergeant Eddie Pope and the rear gunner, Sergeant Les Saunders remained, the latter attempting to act as navigator. They were helped when the fire went out on its own.

They crossed the coast and islands were spotted, some debate taking place as to whether they were in the vicinity of the Scillies or the Isle of Wight. Singleton landed on farmland and he and his two companions were taken aback to find themselves prisoners of German soldiers. They were in Sark which had been occupied since 1940. To locals the Lancaster's landing ground became "the Aeroplane Field".

"We were then taken to a room for interrogation. I was asked questions such as 'Where was your base?' Which type of aircraft were you flying and where was your target? Where were you shot down and who helped you?'

"Predictably, my replies were, I cannot give you that information and quoting the Geneva Convention on the requirement to give only number, rank and name. The others gave the same answers.

"I then heard the lines that were to be caricatured many times in the future but were extremely threatening and sinister given the situation of airmen being captured in civilian clothes. I quote verbatim, 'Huh! So you won't talk, well it is not my job but we have ways and means of making you talk!' We were threatened with torture and the firing squad but we never revealed any details of the people who had helped us. From the mountain village, we were then taken back to Pau, and as I subsequently found out later, spent some time in Gestapo headquarters. Curiously enough, during our short spell there, we were given the best meal in all the time we spent in German hands. Mind you, that wasn't saying very much.

"From Pau, we were taken under escort by train to a civilian prison in Toulouse. During the train journey, another incident of note occurred. We were in a compartment by ourselves with armed German guards when the door opened and a Luftwaffe officer came in. He looked at us and said in English, 'Who are you?'

"At this point, the German soldiers were obviously unhappy but as he was an officer, they were limited in what they could do or say. On being told we were RAF airmen who had been shot down he replied, 'I thought perhaps you were.' He took out a pack of cigarettes, gave us a cigarette each and said 'Good Luck!' before leaving. Had we witnessed an example of the special bond between flying types?"

A recollection by Flight Lieutenant Harry Fisher. He was Wireless Operator in a Stirling of No 218 Squadron, in No 3 Group, flying from Woolfox Lodge, Rutland on the night of April 22/23 1944, with railway installations at Laon, northern France as the target. The aircraft was attacked by a night fighter and the order given to bale out. Five members of the crew did so, but the pilot, Squadron Leader C W Poulter and the Mid Upper Gunner, Flight Sergeant F W Lambert, failed to escape.

Harry Fisher was one of a group of evading airmen captured by German soldiers as they were about to cross into Spain. In August 1944 resistance fighters broke open the prison in which Harry Fisher was held. In September he managed to board a special duties Hudson delivering arms and supplies to the resistance and was flown home.

Ramrod – Similar to a Circus (see that entry), but with the bombers having a specific target to seek to destroy.

Ranks – RAF and Luftwaffe ranks were not precisely equivalent. Some examples of approximate equivalents are:-

Corporal = Gefreiter

Sergeant = Unteroffizier, Unterfeldwebel

Flight Sergeant = Feldwebel

Warrant Officer = Stabsfeldwebel, Oberfeldwebel

Pilot Officer = Leutnant

Flying Officer = Oberleutnant

Flight Lieutenant = Hauptmann

Squadron Leader = Major

Wing Commander = Oberstleutnant

Group Captain = Oberst

Rituals – Many crews had rituals and other superstitions. Urinating on the tail wheel immediately before entering the aircraft for take off was one of the favourite habits. Some carried good luck charms. A Lancaster pilot who had a lucky teddy bear forgot it on one occasion and, as he survived, did not carry it again.

On a good many stations WAAFs and other non-flying personnel would wave aircraft off and perhaps also assemble to welcome them back. However, at Bourn, superstition dictated that people did not turn out in this way.

"Rituals, and superstitions. I prayed a lot, I prayed always before I went on operations. We had our talisman. We took all the WAAF parachute packers out for a pie and a pint, and a little WAAF very kindly and very sweetly got out her purse and gave me a Victorian bun penny, one of the very old coins with Victoria when she was young, with the bun of hair at the back. It had a hole in it. She said, 'Here, take this as a lucky charm for the future' which I did, and I always flew with it. My uncle gave me a silver cigarette case and I never flew without that too. I always kept mine in my breast pocket, over my heart. This was very much a superstition.

"I and many of my friends had girlfriends' stockings too. When you flew you had a white pullover, but you were not allowed to wear a collar and tie because the collars in those days were detachable and if you went in the water the clothing might shrink and suffocate you. So everybody had gay coloured scarves, be they old school scarves, or girlfriends' stockings, which you wore round your neck. There were lots of teddy bears, even teddy bears in flying kit, and things made by wives or girlfriends."

Flight Lieutenant Harry Le Marchant, an Observer.

Royal Air Force Volunteer Reserve (RAFVR) – Organisation founded in 1936 with the prime purpose of providing a pool of additional aircrew for use in the event of war. From the start of the Second World War the RAFVR became the principal route of entry for aircrew into the RAF.

One effect of the pre-war RAFVR was to help extend the recruitment of pilots to a much wider social circle.

Today, in much changed form, the VR continues to support the RAF in a variety of ways.

(With the military build up in Germany) "Desperate, or at the very least, bold and innovative measures were needed and the politicians announced a daring plan in July 1936. Wisely the kernel of the idea had been planted earlier by the air chiefs and quickly taken root at Westminster.

"Young men who did not have to give up their jobs could learn to fly and to fight on week nights, Saturdays and Sundays, and at summer camps. This was to be a citizen's army of the air, part of our national insurance policy, training just in case.

"The call for volunteers went out and thousands stepped forward on the first day. Too many, initially, for the scheme. All over the country there were clerks and engineers, school teachers and shop assistants, bankers, butchers, bakers and even candle stick makers who wanted to wear uniform and fly. Ready in time to defend their country."

From *The Royal Air Force Volunteer Reserve, Memories*, by Wing Commander Alex Dickson.

This pre-war saying is quoted in the same book

"There are three kinds of Air Force Officer ...

The regular who is an officer trying to become a gentleman

The Auxiliary who is a gentleman trying to become an officer

And there is the VR who is neither trying to become both"

Ruhr (Battle Of) – The period March-July 1943 when many attacks were launched against industrial targets situated in the Ruhr region and close by.

Saundby, Air Marshal Sir Robert Henry Magnus Spencer (1896-1971) – Worked briefly for the London and North Western Railway and was commissioned in a territorial battalion of the Royal Warwickshire Regiment. Saundby transferred to the Royal Flying Corps in 1915, seeing action in France as a pilot, being credited with the destruction of nine enemy aircraft.

Back in the UK Saundby received the MC after he had participated in the destruction of Zeppelin L48 in the early hours of June 17 1917, the airship falling near the village of Theburton, Suffolk.

In the immediate post-war RAF "Sandy" Saundby served in Egypt where he met Arthur Harris. Steady progression between the wars included spells as an instructor, participation in the 1927 Hendon air display and tours at the Air Ministry, latterly as Director of Operational Requirements. In this post he showed himself to be an advocate of four-engined bombers.

In the spring of 1940 Saundby was appointed Assistant Chief of the Air Staff responsible for operational requirements and tactics. In November that year he became Senior Air Staff Officer at Bomber Command headquarters.

Air Vice-Marshal Saundby took on the role of Deputy Air Officer Commanding-in-Chief, under Harris, in February 1943, quickly becoming an Air Marshal. He was appointed KBE in the New Year Honours of 1944.

Saundby retired in 1946. He was Chairman of the Royal Air Forces Association and a council member of the Royal Air Force Benevolent Fund.

Screened – Taken off operations at the end of a tour.

Serrate – A radar receiver designed, when fitted to RAF night fighters, to detect German night fighter transmissions from their "Lichtenstein" aircraft interception radar (AI).

Short Stirling – The first four-engined bomber to enter service with the RAF and the earliest to be withdrawn. The Stirling first flew on May 14 1939 and the initial unit to receive operational examples was No 7 Squadron in August 1940. Operations were flown from February 1941 and the Stirling remained in front line service until September 1944. Its other existences included as a transport, troop carrier and glider tug.

Bristol Hercules engines were used and the Stirling could carry up to 14,000lb of bombs.

Pilots found the Stirling a manoeuvrable aircraft but the low ceiling of 16,500 ft sometimes made life difficult for its crews,

A Stirling under construction.

Groundcrew at work on a Short Stirling.

not least when having to fly through, rather than over, the Alps for attacks on targets in Italy. The original intention had been to use the same wings as the manufacturer's Sunderland flying boat, but that would have meant the Stirling would not have fitted into standard RAF hangars, so altitude was sacrificed on that score.

Shuttle Raid – A raid involving landing at a foreign airfield, for example in North Africa, after leaving the target, because of the distance involved. Alternatively, the attack might be launched from overseas.

Sinclair, Sir Archibald Henry Macdonald Bt (1890-1970) – After Eton and Sandhurst Sinclair joined the Life Guards in 1910. He succeeded to the Baronetcy in 1912, on the death of his grandfather. A glamorous and wealthy society figure in his youth, "his good looks, charm and romantic Highland aura were spiced with a touch of daredevilry that led him to experiment with a primitive aircraft that he flew before breakfast, there were few more glamorous young men in Society," wrote Paul Addison for the *Oxford Dictionary of National Biography*. In contrast, in later life he would sometimes be regarded as a rather grey figure.

He formed a close friendship with Winston Churchill and for some months on the Western Front he was Churchill's second in command with the 6th Battalion, Royal Scots Fusiliers. Between 1919 and 1921 he was successively Churchill's personal military secretary at the War Office and his private secretary at the Colonial Office.

In 1922 Sinclair was elected Liberal MP for Caithness and Sutherland. After being Liberal Chief Whip and Secretary of State for Scotland in the National Government led by Ramsay MacDonald, he became Chairman of the Parliamentary Liberal Party in 1935. In September 1939 he declined an offer from Neville Chamberlain, then Prime Minister, to take office. Following Churchill gaining the Premiership on May 10 1940 Sinclair became Secretary of State for Air, finding himself in conflict with the empire-building Lord Beaverbrook, Minister of Aircraft Production.

Sinclair retained his post until 1945 and lost his Parliamentary seat in the General Election of that year. He was created Viscount Thurso in 1952.

Spoof Raids – An operation intended to divert enemy attention from the main raid taking place at the same time.

Squadron – Loosely defined RAF administrative unit, below Group level. Operational squadrons in Bomber Command in the Second World War were usually headed by a Wing Commander, with Squadron Leaders commanding the flights into which a Squadron was divided.

Supreme Headquarters Allied Expeditionary Force (SHAEF) – From April 14 to September 14 1944 Bomber Command was under the control not of the Chief of the Air Staff, but of SHAEF and its leader, General Dwight D Eisenhower, responsible for the invasion of France. Air Chief Marshal Harris reported to Eisenhower through Air Chief Marshal Tedder, the Deputy Supreme Commander.

Harris had argued that his force was not capable of hitting with sufficient accuracy targets such as railway marshalling yards, the destruction of which were crucial to the success of the invasion. In addition he viewed the disruption that would be caused to the strategic offensive as a means of releasing more enemy resources for attacks on invasion targets.

His arguments were probably always doomed to failure but a series of attacks, ordered by CAS, in March 1944, on railway and similar targets was successful and the Harris contention certainly did not survive that. He was allowed to continue attacking Germany, but also had to deal with communications targets nearer to home – described in a directive from Tedder as, "the supreme operation for 1944".

Harris, in fact, got on well with Eisenhower, who was capable of expressing sentiments that resonated well with Harris's views. Harris often attended Commanders-in-Chief meetings discussing Overlord.

Directive by the Supreme Commander to Bomber Command regarding Operation Overlord, the Normandy Offensive.

"The overall mission of the strategical Air Forces remains the progressive destruction and dislocation of the German military, industrial and economic system and the destruction of vital elements of lines of communication. In the execution of this overall mission the immediate objective is first the destruction of German air combat strength by the successful prosecution of the combined bomber offensive. Our re-entry to the Continent constitutes the supreme operation for 1944; all possible support must therefore be afforded to the Allied

Attack in the area of Bruges, Belgium with bombs bursting around a canal and railway lines. Attacks on transport installations contributed to the success of the invasion of Europe.

armies by our Air Forces to assist them in establishing themselves in the lodgement areas.

"The first pre-requisite of success in the maintenance of the combined bomber offensive and of our re-entry on the Continent is an overall reduction of the enemy's air combat strength and particularly his air fighter strength. The primary role of our Air Forces in the European and Mediterranean theatres is therefore to secure and maintain air superiority.

"Our armies will also require maximum possible assistance on the ground preparatory to the actual assault. This can best be given by interfering with rail communications, particularly as affecting the enemy movements and concentrations in the Overlord area. A further Directive covering the employment of the strategical Air Forces during the assault period and succeeding land operations will be issued in due course.

"The particular mission of the strategical Air Forces prior to the Overlord assault is:-

To deplete the German air force and particularly the German fighter forces and to destroy and disorganise the facilities supporting them.

To destroy and disrupt the enemy's rail communications, particularly those affecting the enemy's movement towards the Overlord lodgement area."

Tallboy – A 12,000lb deep penetration bomb developed by the Vickers engineer Barnes Wallis. It was designed to achieve an "earthquake" effect when dropped from Lancasters against buried targets or those that were extremely strongly built. Key issues were the creation of a shape that would reach high speeds in the air, aiding penetration and a strong casing that would survive the penetration process.

On the night of June 8/9 1944, the Tallboy was put to use for the first time after it was realised that German Panzer forces heading towards the Allied forces in Normandy would

Lifting a Tallboy bomb.

shortly pass through the Saumur railway tunnel near the town of that name between the Loire and Thouet rivers. The operation was carried out by No 617 Squadron using both Lancasters carrying Tallboys and others carrying conventional bombs. The target was marked by a Mosquito flown by Wing Commander G L Cheshire, the squadron's CO.

Such was the haste with which the attack had to be planned and implemented that some aircrew earmarked to take part needed to be retrieved from a cricket match.

Despite the speed, the operation was a complete success – the tunnel was blocked and the arrival of the Panzers in the battle area seriously delayed. No aircraft were lost.

From then on Tallboys were used against a range of targets including, sites associated with the German V-1 and V-2 weapons, as well as docks housing U-boats and E-boats, the large German ships *Tirpitz* and *Lutzow* and viaducts.

Target for Tonight – Highly praised British documentary film made in 1941, with one Wellington and its crew as stars. The director was Harry Watt.

The Bomber Will Always Get Through – Words often quoted (though he did not originate them) from a speech made by Stanley Baldwin in the House of Commons on November 10 1932. Baldwin was three times Prime Minister, but at this juncture he was Lord President of the Council.

The context was a debate springing from a motion on disarmament put down by Clement Attlee, then Deputy Leader of the Labour Party.

Although the words that have gone down in history have often been portrayed as a counsel of despair and came to symbolise much Government and RAF policy as the thirties wore on, Baldwin also spoke of the possibility of the abolition of bombers (as, he said, other terrible weapons had not been used in the Great War) and of the international control of civil aviation, to address the risk that civil aircraft might be used as makeshift bombers in time of war.

There was much truth in what Baldwin said, when he said it, but the development of forms of defence such as radar produced a rather more complicated situation as both the RAF and the Luftwaffe found in 1939/40.

At the outset of his speech Baldwin claimed that disarmament would not stop war, rather it was a matter of the will to achieve peace.

Later he said:-

"I have studied these matters myself for many years. My duty has made me Chairman for five years of the Committee of Imperial Defence. I have sat continuously for 10 years on that Committee, except during the period when the present Opposition were in power, and there is no subject that interests me more deeply nor which is more fraught with the ultimate well or ill being of the human race.

"What the world suffers from is a sense of fear, a want of confidence; and it is a fear held instinctively and without knowledge very often. But my own view — and I have slowly and deliberately come to this conclusion — is that there is no one thing that is more responsible for that fear — and I am speaking of what Mr Attlee called the common people, of whom I am the chief— than the fear of the air.

"Up to the time of the last War civilians were exempt from the worst perils of war. They suffered sometimes from hunger, sometimes from the loss of sons and relatives serving in the Army. But now, in addition to this, they suffered from the constant fear not only of being killed themselves, but, what is perhaps worse for a man, of seeing his wife and children killed from the air. These feelings exist among the ordinary people throughout the whole of the civilized world, but I doubt if many of those who have that fear realise one or two things with reference to the cause of that fear.

That is the appalling speed which the air has brought into

German personnel inspect the remains of a downed Bomber Command aircraft.

modern warfare; the speed of the attack. The speed of the attack, compared with the attack of an army, is as the speed of a motor-car to that of a four-in-hand. In the next war you will find that any town within reach of an aerodrome can be bombed within the first five minutes of war to an extent inconceivable in the last War, and the question is, whose morale will be shattered quickest by that preliminary bombing?

I think it is well also for the man in the street to realise that there is no power on earth that can protect him from being bombed, whatever people may tell him. *The bomber will always get through* and it is very easy to understand that if you realise the area of space. Take any large town you like on this island or on the Continent within reach of an aerodrome. For the defence of that town and its suburbs you have to split up the air into sectors for defence. Calculate that the bombing aeroplanes will be at least 20,000ft high in the air, and perhaps higher, and it is a matter of mathematical calculation that you will have sectors of from 10 to hundreds of cubic miles.

Imagine 100 cubic miles covered with cloud and fog, and you can calculate how many aeroplanes you would have to throw into that to have much chance of catching odd aeroplanes as they fly through it. It cannot be done, and there is no expert in Europe who will say that it can. The only defence is in offence, which means that you have got to kill more women and children more quickly than the enemy if you want to save yourselves. I mention that so that people may realise what is waiting for them when the next war comes."

The resonance of the speech in official and public minds lay partly in the experience of the First World War when relatively small numbers of German bombers and airships scattered bombs over London and the surrounding areas. The total number of deaths in London from bombing between 1915 and 1918 was 670, but the impact on a population totally unused to this form of warfare was far greater. Incidents such as the deaths of 18 children at Upper North Road council primary school in Poplar in 1917 inevitably attracted much attention.

When a raid seemed a possibility thousands crowded into underground stations, as they would do in the second great conflict and sometimes they were difficult to shift when the threat was no longer apparent. Years later this would be remembered when official policy was against "deep shelters".

With all this in mind, as well as the impact on civilians of bombing during the Spanish Civil War, official thinking in the late 1930s contemplated immediate bombing of London if war came, mass panic and rioting and 58,000 deaths in the first 24 hours.

Although Viscount Trenchard, the great figure in the founding of the RAF, had ceased to be Chief of the Air Staff in 1930, he remained active both behind the scenes and sometimes venturing on stage. Air Ministry policy continued to reflect his view that a large British bomber force was a great deterrent and, even if that proved not to be the case, the bombers could inflict vast damage on the enemy economy.

"We thought of air warfare in 1938 rather as people think of nuclear power today," wrote former Prime Minister Harold Macmillan (later Earl of Stockton) in 1966.

Thousand Bomber Raids – In 1942 Arthur Harris inherited a Command under much criticism. A plan to demonstrate what could be done became the "Thousand Bomber" attack on Cologne (Operation Millennium, May 30/31 1942) with later operations against Essen and Bremen. However, the figure of 1,000 was not quite reached on the later attacks. Originally Hamburg had been the intended opening target, but meteorological forecasts led to a change of plan.

The Main Force of bombers could provide nowhere near enough aircraft, though the problem was initially eased by a promise of 250 bombers from Coastal Command. When the

The memorial to Flying Officer Leslie Manser VC in the vicinity of the spot where his Avro Manchester crashed on the Thousand Bomber attack on Cologne. Photograph by Fik Geuens.

Royal Navy refused to allow this contribution to be made, efforts had to be redoubled to find aircraft and crews from Heavy Conversion Units, Operational Training Units and other training establishments. Much of the credit for the fact that 1,047 aircraft eventually set out for Cologne lay with the work of Air Vice-Marshal Saundby, Harris's Senior Air Staff Officer.

Supporting intruder operations were laid on by aircraft from Bomber, Fighter and Army Co-operation Commands.

The attack was deemed a success, with around 870 bombers attacking the main target and the RAF casualty rate was not as high as had been feared with 52 aircraft and crews failing to return. An example of the extent to which unusual sources were plundered for aircraft and crews was the Wellington 1A from the Central Gunnery School, which was shot down by a night fighter and crashed in the Netherlands, with the loss of all but one of its crew. It has been suggested that this was the last Wellington 1A to be lost on bomber operations.

In Cologne 3,300 buildings were destroyed, less than 500 people killed, according to German records, but a very high proportion of the population left the city in the aftermath of the raid.

As a result of Operation Millennium both the reputation of the Command and its morale improved.

Tirpitz – Bismarck class battleship of the German Navy that saw little action (and spent much time holed up along the Norwegian coast) but was regarded as a major threat to shipping by the Allies. The need to put the *Tirpitz* out of action led to a number of attacks by Bomber Command, after efforts by the Royal Navy, including attack by midget submarines and by the Fleet Air Arm, had not produced the great prize.

Bomber Command went into action against the *Tirpitz* in Kaa Fjord, Norway, on September 15 1944 (Operation Paravane). Flying from Russia, Lancasters of Nos 617 and 9 Squadrons, led by Wing Commander Willie Tait of 617, attacked with Tallboys and mines. Their approach was detected and the ship's excellent smokescreen system deployed, but one Tallboy did cause severe damage, rendering the ship unseaworthy. However, this was not realised by British intelligence and further attacks took place.

The ship was moved to Tromso, bringing it within range of Lancasters fitted with additional fuel tanks and flying from Lossiemouth in Scotland. The relative shortness of the Lossiemouth runway was overcome by fitting a more powerful variant of the Merlin engine and stripping out much weight including the mid upper turret.

Operation Obviate was flown from Lossiemouth on October 28 by the same squadrons, but sea clouds protected the ship and only near misses were scored. The one casualty of this sortie was, "E Easy", the No 617 Squadron Lancaster flown by Flying Officer Bill Carey, RAAF. Badly damaged by flak, during six runs over the target and unable to return to Scotland, the aircraft crash-landed in a Swedish bog injuring the pilot. He and his crew eventually returned to Britain.

On November 12 the squadrons went to Norway again in an attack designated Operation Catechism. Surprise was achieved and direct hits were scored with a number of Tallboys, one of which penetrated the ship's magazine. The threat of the *Tirpitz* was over.

Tommies – Sobriquet often applied by Germans to the RAF airmen who flew overhead.

The name had long been used in the British Army to denote an ordinary soldier. Some sources claim that it was current in the mid 18th century, others that it derives from the use of "Thomas Atkins" as a typical name in official documents from 1815.

During the 1890s Rudyard Kipling published the poem *Tommy* and there was a music hall song, *Private Tommy Atkins*.

In the First World War, "Tommy" was much in use in the German Army when referring to British soldiers and was shouted across no man's land when attempts were being made to establish communication.

The term "Terror Fliegers" was also used, though this was not universal. German propaganda often referred to "Terror Bombing".

"We never used that expression ('Terror Fliegers'). We said, 'The Tommies are coming tonight.'" Edith Cripps (nee Martens) speaking in 1980. She had spent the war as a nursing orderly in the town of Heiligenhaus, close to Dusseldorf and Essen.

Tour – Word commonly used to denote the number of operational hours or sorties an airman had to undertake before he could expect a rest.

Early in the war the normal end of a tour came after 200 hours of operational flying. It was contended that this definition could be used to advantage by less enthusiastic crews who did not always press on to the target when they might have done. So the normal requirement, from early 1943, became 30 operational sorties, with the onus on the squadron CO using as much photographic evidence as possible. A second tour would consist of 20 sorties.

Problems arose when there was the requirement, in 1944, to attack targets in France and the low countries in support of the invasion. These attacks occurred frequently in a short period, quickly pushing airmen towards the end of their tours and they were considered "soft" targets as well.

There was much disharmony when the solution was announced – that such targets would only count as one third of an operation and compromises were effected.

A man who had finished his tour was "tour expired".

United States Army Air Force (USAAF) – The USAAF came into being on June 20 1941, as a component of the United States Army, though its antecedents dated back to 1907. The immediate predecessor organisation (and one which co-existed for a time) was the US Army Air Corps. A separate United States Air Force (USAF) was formed in September 1947 and replaced the USAAF.

The Eighth Air Force, part of the USAAF, began to arrive in Britain in 1942. Contrary to claims that are sometimes made, there was immediate co-operation between Bomber Command and the Americans, whose role developed as daylight bombing, while the RAF maintained the fight at night.

Initially the senior US airman in Britain was Brigadier General Ira C Eaker, a 46 year-old Texan who had learned to fly while serving in the US Army in the First World War. At the invitation of Arthur Harris, Eaker and his staff initially used office accommodation at the Bomber Command HQ at High Wycombe. British personnel were loaned to Eaker to advise on a range of issues and RAF and WAAF clerks assisted his administration. Eaker then established himself at the newly-requisitioned Wycombe Abbey School. Modifications at the all girls school included the construction of an underground bunker and a hutted encampment.

Early bases were north west of Huntingdon, but the eventual solution was to make much of East Anglia the domain of the Eighth Air Force.

For the rest of the war co-operation between Bomber Command and its United States counterpart continued, though the USAAF mainly claimed to be attacking specific targets (however widely bombs might fall) as opposed to conducting area bombing.

Very Light – A pistol used for signalling, by creating a pyrotechnic display when fired. Its invention, early in the 20th century, was attributed to Edward W Very, American naval officer.

A Vickers Wellington MK 1A in flight.

Vickers Wellington – A twin-engined medium bomber that was a mainstay of Bomber Command in the early years of the war. It was particularly noted for its "geodetic" construction (already utilised in the Vickers Wellesley), using a criss-crossing metal mesh, intended to add greatly to the strength of the fuselage.

The type first flew in 1936 and spectators at that year's Hendon air display found themselves watching an aircraft that seemed far ahead of existing RAF bombers such as the biplane Handley Page Heyford and Vickers Virginia, the latter having been in operational service with the RAF since 1924.

A Vickers Wellington and aircrew of No 149 Squadron at RAF Mildenhall, 1940.

An early belief that the type could be effective in daylight operations flying in strict formation proved erroneous, with heavy casualties being suffered. Unsealed fuel tanks were a particular issue when under attack from Luftwaffe fighters.

The prolific Mk 1C version had two Bristol Pegasus engines, two 0.303 machine guns each in the nose and tail turrets, two in beam positions and was capable of carrying a bomb load of up to 4,500 lb.

A propaganda exercise staged at the Vickers shadow factory at Broughton near Chester, involved the manufacture of Wellington LN 514 in just over 24 hours. This was filmed by the Ministry of Information for showing on newsreels.

Wellingtons saw much service in Coastal Command and in the Middle and Far East.

The aircraft acquired the universal nickname, "Wimpy" derived from the character J Wellington Wimpy in the *Popeye* cartoons.

Production of the Wellington outlived the war and it continued in RAF service, in a training role, into the 1950s.

A Wellington Rear Gunner has less than happy memories, "Gun turrets by Vickers – bloody awful. Two guns fixed to central mounting rotated, but gunner's seat fixed. This required acrobatics by air gunner since his seat was fixed facing rear, whilst guns turned taking sights away from gunner who had to lean over and twist to get his head in line with gunsights. A beam shot was almost impossible."

Victoria Cross – Britain's highest decoration for gallantry. Queen Victoria signed a Royal Warrant to institute the award on January 29 1856.

During the Second World War 19 aircrew serving with Bomber Command earned the VC.

In the following list (P) indicates a posthumous decoration. Dates given are those of the acts leading to the awards. The decorations were not gazetted in that order. For example, the VC earned by Sergeant Jackson in April 1944 was not announced until October 26 1945, after other survivors of his crew had returned from PoW camps and signed witness statements.

Flight Lieutenant R A B Learoyd, August 12 1940, attack on Dortmund-Ems Canal

Roderick "Babe" Learoyd was the pilot of the fifth Hampden in a formation attacking this heavily defended target. He flew through intense flak and despite his aircraft being hit and coned by searchlights his attack was successful. He flew the badly damaged aircraft back to Scampton and circled until daylight as he did not consider that a landing in darkness should be attempted when the extent of the damage was unknown.

Flight Lieutenant "Babe" Learoyd, was a Hampden pilot who earned the VC in 1940. His ironic nickname was a reference to his exceptional height.

Sergeant J Hannah, September 15 1940, attack on barges at Antwerp

John Hannah was the WOP/AG in a Hampden of No 83 Squadron, flown by Pilot Officer Arthur Connor and tasked to attack German invasion barges at Antwerp. During a second run over the target area the aircraft was set on fire by flak, with ammunition exploding.

Hannah fought the fire, suffering severe burns as he did so and, as the other two crew members had baled out, helped the pilot navigate the aircraft back to Scampton. Connor, who would be lost in November 1940, received the DFC and Sergeant D A E Hayhurst, the Observer/Bomb Aimer, who had become a PoW, was awarded the DFM.

Wing Commander H I Edwards, July 4 1941, attack on Bremen

Hughie Edwards led a daylight attack by Nos 105 and 107 Squadrons. He flew through heavy flak and balloon cables and released his bombs over the docks. His aircraft was hit nearly 20 times and the air gunner, Sergeant G Quinn, wounded. Quinn received a bar to the DFM and the observer, Pilot Officer Ramsay, was awarded the DFC. Edwards was much later Governor of Western Australia and received a knighthood.

Sergeant J A Ward, RNZAF, July 7 1941, raid on Munster

Jimmy Ward was second pilot in the No 75 Squadron Wellington flown by Squadron Leader R P Widdowson. On the return flight the aircraft was attacked by a Messerschmitt Bf 110; although he was wounded, the rear gunner, Sergeant A J R Box, shot this aircraft down. Ward was ordered to try to put out a fire in the starboard wing. After he and two other crew members had failed using an extinguisher, Ward climbed out to the wing root, while tied to one of his comrades and managed to reduce the fire using a cockpit cover canvas. He returned inside and the Wellington reached England. Widdowson was awarded the DFC and Box the DFM.

Two months later Ward, flying as skipper, was not one of the two survivors when his Wellington fell to flak over Hamburg.

"I had a good look at the fire and I thought there was a sporting chance of reaching it by getting out through the astrodome, then down the side of the fuselage and out on to the wing. Joe, the navigator, said he thought it was crazy. There was a rope there; just the normal length of rope attached to the rubber dinghy to stop it drifting away from the aircraft when it's released on the water."

Sergeant Jimmy Ward, broadcasting anonymously on the BBC.

Squadron Leader J D Nettleton, April 17 1942, attack on M.A.N. diesel engine factory Augsberg

John Nettleton, of No 44 Squadron, defied fighter attacks and heavy flak to bomb the factory, having flown to southern Germany in daylight. Seven of the 12 Lancasters on the operation were lost. Nettleton did not return from an attack on Turin on July 12/13 1943.

Flying Officer L T Manser (P), May 30/31 1942, operation against Cologne

Before joining the RAF Leslie Manser had been rejected by both the Army and Royal Navy. On the Thousand Bomber raid to Cologne he was the pilot of an Avro Manchester of No 50 Squadron. Over the target the aircraft was hit by flak and the rear gunner (Sergeant B W Naylor) wounded, the port engine then caught fire. Seeking to reach England the crew jettisoned everything that they could. Eventually, with speed close to stalling point, the skipper ordered the crew to abandon the aircraft. The second pilot, Sergeant Baveystock, attempted to clip on the pilot's parachute, but Manser shouted, "For God's sake get out". Immediately after this order was obeyed the Manchester crashed close to the Belgian village of Bree, with Manser still inside. The rest of the crew survived and all but the navigator, injured when he hit the ground, evaded.

Pilot Officer R H Middleton, RAAF, (P) November 28/29 1942, attack on Fiat factories, Turin

While approaching the target the Stirling of which Rawdon "Ron" Middleton was skipper was hit by flak, he was badly wounded and other members of the crew were also hit. The bombs were released and, with his windscreen shattered, Middleton set course for England. Over the Kent coast he ordered his crew to bale out – the Stirling crashed into the sea off Dymchurch and there were five survivors, all of whom received the DFC or DFM.

Squadron Leader L H Trent, RNZAF, May 3 1943, attack on Amsterdam power station

Len Trent led an attack by 12 Venturas of No 487 Squadron, not knowing that many German fighters were airborne in proximity of

the target as the German governor of Holland was visiting Haarlem. On the run in Trent shot down a Bf 109. His aircraft reached the target and dropped its bombs, the only aircraft to do so. The Ventura was then hit and became uncontrollable, Trent ordered the crew to bale out, although only the navigator, Flight Lieutenant V Phillips, survived. The aircraft blew up and Trent was thrown out. He landed by parachute and was taken prisoner.

Wing Commander G P Gibson, May 16/17 1943, attack on dams in western Germany

Guy Gibson formed and commanded No 617 Squadron and led it during the attack on the dams. After releasing his mine at the Mohne, he flew his Lancaster as a distraction for the German gunners while other aircraft attacked. Gibson was killed in August 1944 flying a Mosquito and acting as master bomber in an attack on Rheydt and Munchen Gladbach. (See also entry for Dam Busters).

Flight Sergeant A L Aaron (P), August 12 1943, operation against Turin

Arthur "Art" Aaron was a pilot with No 218 Squadron operating Stirlings from Downham Market. He had been awarded the DFM after completing an attack and bringing his aircraft home despite severe flak damage. On the night of August 12/13 1943 the target was Turin. Approaching the objective the aircraft was badly damaged, apparently by fire from another Stirling, though the VC citation would attribute this to a German night fighter.

Aaron was terribly wounded in the face and had one arm almost severed, the navigator, Sergeant Bill Brennan, was killed and the aircraft went into a dive. Control was regained by the bomb aimer (Sergeant Allen Larden) and the flight engineer (Sergeant Malcolm Mitchem). Larden continued to fly the aircraft and Aaron, though unable to speak, scratched a message telling him to head for England. The bombs were jettisoned in the vicinity of the harbour at Spezia. For a time the mid upper gunner Sergeant Richmond took the controls with Aaron still conscious and asking to be informed of the situation. Eventually it was decided to make for Bone in Algeria. Larden took over in the pilot's seat. Aaron had been unconscious but insisted on resuming control for the landing. He aborted two landings and was about to abort a third, seeming unable to understand shouts from the flight engineer that they were virtually out of fuel. Larden forcibly regained control and achieved a belly-landing. It was discovered that there was still one bomb on board.

Arthur Aaron died about nine hours after landing. Larden received the CGM and Mitchem and Sergeant "Jimmy" Guy, the wireless operator, the DFM.

Flight Lieutenant W Reid, November 3 1943, operation to Dusseldorf

As Bill Reid's Lancaster crossed the Dutch coast outward bound it was attacked by a Messerschmitt Bf 110, the windscreen was smashed and Reid was wounded. He continued with the sortie but the aircraft then suffered an attack by a Focke Wulf Fw 190 – this time Reid was hit again, Flight Sergeant Jefferies, the navigator was killed, Sergeant Mann (wireless operator) was badly wounded and Flight Sergeant Norris (Flight Engineer) was hit. The oxygen and hydraulic systems were ruptured and the compass was unserviceable. Reid pressed on to the target and bombed. On the way home, with Reid weakened by his wounds, he was assisted in flying the Lancaster by Norris and Sergeant Rolton the bomb aimer. Eventually the aircraft was landed at the USAAF base at Shipdham, Norfolk. Mann died the next day. Norris received the CGM and a DFM was awarded to Flight Sergeant "Joe" Emerson, the rear gunner. The crew were with No 61 Squadon.

Bill Reid later flew with No 617 Squadron. In July 1944 his Lancaster was struck by a bomb from another aircraft while attacking the V weapon storage site at Rilly La Montagne near Rheims. Reid was one of two survivors and became a prisoner. Les Rolton was amongst those lost.

Pilot Officer C J Barton (P), March 30 1944, attack on Nuremburg

Cyril "Cy" Barton was the pilot of a Halifax on No 578 Squadron on an operation in which Bomber Command suffered very heavy losses. Approaching the target the aircraft was attacked by two

night fighters and the starboard inner engine caught fire; misunderstanding a morse signal, the navigator, wireless operator and bomb aimer baled out. Barton nonetheless pressed on and bombed, though possibly Schweinfurt rather than Nuremburg. He then set course for home, but, with no navigator, seems to have flown parallel to the English coast. Eventually, over land and with fuel almost exhausted, he ordered the remaining members of his crew to adopt crash positions. At Ryhope near Sunderland, the aircraft struck some cottages and one person on the ground nearby was killed – all the men in the aircraft survived the crash, but Cy Barton died shortly afterwards.

"In gallantly completing his last mission in the face of almost impossible odds, this officer displayed unsurpassed courage and devotion to duty." From the citation for Pilot Officer Barton's Victoria Cross.

Sergeant N C Jackson, April 26 1944, raid on Schweinfurt

A former aero engine fitter, Norman Jackson had remustered as a Flight Engineer. He had completed his tour with No 106 Squadron, including one operation when he had stood in for a flight engineer who was ill. He volunteered for a 31st sortie with his regular crew, led by a Newfoundlander, Flying Officer Fred Mifflin. The target was Schweinfurt.

After dropping its bombs the Lancaster was attacked by a night fighter and the starboard inner engine burst into flames, threatening nearby petrol tanks. Jackson volunteered to climb outside the aircraft, his parachute already deployed and try to put out the fire with an extinguisher. He managed to reduce the fire, but the fighter made another attack, Jackson was wounded and burned and fell from the wing, with his parachute damaged and on fire. Crewmates pushed out the parachute lines they had been holding and he landed heavily damaging both his ankles. He was eventually taken prisoner and subjected to rough treatment by his immediate captors and civilians.

The aircraft crashed after four more of the crew escaped by parachute, but Mifflin (whose DFC, already in the pipeline, was announced shortly afterwards) and the rear gunner, Flight Sergeant Hugh Johnson, were killed.

Warrant Officer A C Mynarski, RCAF (P), June 12 1944, attack on marshalling yards at Cambrai

Flying with No 419, an RCAF squadron, Andrew Mynarski was mid upper gunner in a Lancaster crew of six Canadians and one Englishman, the flight engineer, Sergeant Roy Vigars. The pilot was Flying Officer Arthur de Breyne. The target was to be attacked from only 2,000 ft. Mynarski was unaware of the fact that he had been commissioned the previous day, though his citation for the VC would still refer to him as a Warrant Officer.

As the aircraft closed in on the target it was attacked by a Junkers Ju 88 night fighter. Both port engines were put out of action and a major fire broke out. The rear gunner, Flying Officer George Brophy, was trapped in his turret. Although the pilot had ordered the crew to bale out, Mynarski made his way through the flames to try to rescue his fellow gunner. Despite his clothes being on fire he made several attempts to release Brophy from the jammed turret, but eventually accepted Brophy's urging that he should escape. He jumped with his parachute on fire and died shortly after landing, notwithstanding the efforts of French civilians to save him. Remarkably, Brophy survived when the Lancaster crashed, as did the rest of the crew who had baled out.

Group Captain G L Cheshire, air operations June 1940-July 1944

In the First World War a number of airmen were awarded the VC to mark extended periods of operational fortitude and achievement. Leonard Cheshire was the only such case in the Second World War. He flew his first operational sortie in June 1940 as second pilot in a Whitley of No 102 Squadron and had achieved his 100th in Bomber Command four years later.

His citation noted that, "In four years of fighting against the bitterest opposition he maintained standards of outstanding personal achievement, his successful operations being the result of careful planning, brilliant execution and supreme contempt for danger – for example on one occasion he flew his P-51 Mustang in slow 'figures of eight' above a target obscured by low cloud, to act as a bomb-aiming mark for his squadron. Cheshire displayed the courage and determination of an exceptional leader.

The citation paid particular attention to the attack on Munich in April 1944 when Cheshire, in a Mosquito, flew through searchlights and heavy flak to place markers accurately from 700 feet.

Later Cheshire flew as an observer of the operation when an atomic bomb was dropped on the Japanese city of Nagasaki.

His distinguished post-war career is perhaps remembered most for his efforts for the sick, most prominently the founding of the Cheshire Homes. He became a member of the Order of Merit in 1981 and a peer in 1991.

"'If I am good enough to fight and fly with these men I am certainly good enough to drink with them," a comment by Cheshire after he was criticised for drinking in a saloon bar with NCOs, quoted in the *Oxford Dictionary of National Biography*.

Squadron Leader I W Bazalgette (P), August 4 1944, attack on V-1 storage depot at Trossy St Maximin

Ian Bazalgette was flying on his 55th operation in a Lancaster of No 635 Squadron, part of the PFF. His rear gunner was Pilot Officer Doug Cameron who had also been part of "Ron" Middleton's crew when Middleton earned a posthumous VC. The aircraft of the deputy master bomber, Flight Lieutenant R W Beveridge, had already been shot down, with no survivors, when Bazalgette began his run over the target with markers.

His aircraft was hit by flak, both starboard engines put out of action and a fire started; the bomb aimer, Flight Lieutenant I A Hibberd, was badly wounded and the mid upper gunner, Flight Sergeant V V Leeder, became unconscious through the effects of the fire.

Bazalgette dropped his markers, but eventually ordered the crew to bale out. Four did so and avoided capture until the liberation of the area they were in. The skipper remained with the aircraft to try to save Hibberd and Leeder. He landed on the outskirts of the village of Senantes, but the Lancaster exploded and all three men inside died.

Squadron Leader R A M Palmer (P), December 23 1944, raid on marshalling yards, Cologne

After completing one operational tour on Wellingtons and spending three years as an instructor Bob Palmer was posted to No 109 Squadron in the PFF in January 1944. He went on to earn the DFC and bar and to achieve over 100 sorties. On December 23 1944, flying in a Lancaster, he was Master Bomber for a daylight operation against the Gremberg marshalling yard, Cologne. Approaching the target Palmer took no evasive action in flying through heavy flak that set fire to two of his engines. He released his bombs on the target, the signal for the following aircraft to bomb. Immediately afterwards the burning Lancaster crashed, with only the rear gunner, Warrant Officer Yeulatt, escaping by parachute.

Flight Sergeant G Thompson (P), January 1 1945, attack on Dortmund-Ems Canal

George Thompson was the wireless operator in the No 9 Squadron Lancaster crew of Flying Officer Harry Denton, a New Zealander. On January 1 1945 a dawn attack on the Dortmund-Ems canal was mounted. Immediately after Denton's bomb aimer, Flight Sergeant Ron Goebel, had released the load, the aircraft was hit by shells and set on fire, the flames attacking both turrets. Thompson reached the unconscious mid upper gunner, Sergeant Ernie Potts, whose clothing was on fire, and carried Potts past a large hole in the fuselage to relative safety. Thompson then made his way to the rear turret and assisted Sergeant "Taffy" Price, also badly burned, to where Potts was lying. By this time terribly burned, with much of his clothing gone, Thompson made his way forward to warn the pilot that the gunners were incapable of baling out.

Further flak hit the Lancaster and then Denton was encouraged by the arrival of a number of Spitfires which formated on the stricken bomber. As he attempted to land, one of the fighters flew in front to warn of power cables. Denton managed to lift the Lancaster over them. On landing near the Dutch village of Heesch, the aircraft broke up. Price died the next day and Thompson three weeks later after suffering from pneumonia.

"Flight Sergeant Thompson, by now almost exhausted, felt that his duty was not yet done. He must report the fate of the crew to the captain. He made the perilous journey back through the burning fuselage, clinging to the sides with his burnt hands to get across the hole in the floor. The flow of cold air caused him intense pain and frost-bite developed. So pitiful was his condition that his captain failed to recognise him. Still, his only concern was for the two gunners he had left in the rear of the aircraft. He was given such attention as was possible until a crash-landing was made some forty minutes later." – extract from George Thompson's VC citation as published in the *London Gazette.*

"Jolly good landing skipper," reported remark by George Thompson to Harry Denton immediately after they came down.

Captain E Swales, SAAF (P), February 23 1945, operation against railway junction at Pforzheim

Ted Swales was serving with No 582 Squadron in the PFF. He had been awarded the DFC after evading five fighters on the operation that resulted in a posthumous VC for Bob Palmer; one of the fighters was claimed as destroyed and two damaged.

Swales was Master Bomber for the attack on February 23 1945 against a rail junction, the destruction of which was considered vital. Near the target the Lancaster flown by Swales was hit by fire from a night fighter and lost one engine. Swales pressed on, released his TIs and began to circle the target to give instructions. Another fighter attacked and a second engine was lost, but Swales continued to fly over the target. Satisfied that the attack was a success, he eventually set course for England with no instruments. Over Allied territory the Lancaster went into a spin and the order to abandon the aircraft was given. Everybody except the pilot escaped. He was still at the controls when the aircraft exploded immediately after the last of his crew had jumped.

Barnes Wallis – he contributed the bouncing bomb and much else to the war effort.

Wallis, Sir Barnes Neville (1887-1979) – Son of a general practitioner, he attended Haberdashers' Aske's Hatcham Boys' School in south London and then Christ's Hospital. He was indentured to the Thames Engineering Works and then to the naval shipbuilder J S White of Cowes, Isle of Wight.

From 1913 Wallis worked for Vickers on airships. In 1919 he suffered a nervous breakdown and in 1921 he was laid off. He studied for and gained an external degree at London University and taught maths in Switzerland. Then another opening presented itself at Vickers and he was also commissioned in the TA. During the years that followed he was most famously associated with the design of the successful airship R100. He began to develop his ideas on geodetic design, suffered a second breakdown and also became more and more involved in aircraft design.

Geodetic principles were applied to the Wellesley and then the Wellington. The Warwick bomber followed, but this had been overtaken by the Halifax and Stirling and its most common roles became transport and anti-submarine reconnaissance. A number of prototypes of the four-engined Windsor bomber were built but the project was cancelled. With all these designs it is often debated how much credit should be awarded to Wallis and how much to R K "Rex" Pierson, the long serving Vickers Chief Designer who oversaw all the design work.

Wallis spent much time considering how the German economy might be damaged to the detriment of its war effort and focussed on devising a weapon to breach major German dams, though the concept of attacking the economy via the dams was not his. He was eventually brilliantly successful in creating the "bouncing bomb" used by No 617 Squadron of Bomber Command in 1943. The large Tallboy and Grand Slam bombs used to considerable effect in the latter days of the war were also to the credit of Wallis.

After the war Wallis continued for a quarter of a century to work at Vickers on a series of radical designs, often seeing politicians and bureaucrats as people who obstructed him, a theme that received prominent exposure in the book and film, *The Dam Busters*. He was knighted in 1968.

War Correspondents – A significant number of journalists acting as war correspondents flew on bombing operations. They included the celebrated BBC figure, Richard Dimbleby who completed about 20 operations, despite claiming to dislike flying and to be frequently sick.

In September 1943 BBC recording engineer Reg Pidsley (left) and correspondent Wynford Vaughan-Thomas were photographed as they were about to take off for Berlin.

Dimbleby's colleague, Wynford Vaughan-Thomas was another who reported on Bomber Command's war. In September 1943, for instance, he and recording engineer Reg Pidsley joined the crew of Lancaster "F for Freddie" of No 207 Squadron for the trip to Berlin.

Vaughan-Thomas reported:-

"As we near the city it seems to be ringed by a wall of searchlights. There are hundreds of them in cones and clusters .... a wall of light with very few breaks and behind that wall the city itself – a pool of fiercer light, glowing red and green and blue. Flak from the guns is coming up in a steady stream. There are millions of flares hanging in the sky; the ground seems to be eaten up by fire. —— We are running straight into the most gigantic display of fireworks in the world."

"F for Freddie" survived an attack by a night fighter, but Vaughan-Thomas witnessed the loss of another Lancaster. "I looked behind and saw the shattered wings and the beginning of the headlong descent into the burning chaos below," he told his audience.

The American correspondent Edward R Murrow flew with both the USAAF and the RAF. As he recorded after the war, one of his difficulties was understanding the British way of expressing things.

He found himself over Berlin in a Lancaster coned and corkscrewing. The pilot ordered, "Window like mad". It was not until Murrow was safely back in Blighty that the courtesy of the Bomb Aimer over the intercom struck him as eccentrically British – "Mr Murrow, could you please pass me another package of windows" had been his request.

Some correspondents did not return. In the Berlin 1939-45 War Cemetery is the grave of Norman Stockton of the Sydney Sun, who was in a Lancaster of No 460 Squadron on December 2 1943 which exploded after being attacked by a night fighter. Buried with him are the Pilot, Pilot Officer J H J English, RAAF, Sergeant A G Cole (Wireless Operator) and the two air gunners, Flight Sergeant I Rodin, RCAF and Flight Sergeant A E Kan, RAAF. Three crew members survived as PoWs – Sergeant W L Miller (Flight Engineer), Pilot Officer N J Anderson, RAAF (Navigator) and Flight Sergeant A W Catty (Bomb Aimer).

Window – Strips of aluminium foil on black paper which, when dropped in considerable quantities from Bomber Command aircraft interfered with German radar on the ground and in the air.

Although Window had been available long before it was not authorised for use until July 1943 because of fears that if the Germans started using it too, the defence of the United Kingdom would be significantly weakened. Eventually Winston Churchill gave the go ahead, allegedly with the words, "Very well. Let us open the window". Shortly afterwards Window was used to considerable effect on Operation Gomorrah, the major attack on Hamburg.

It is now known that the Japanese had deployed a version of Window in the Pacific two months before the first RAF use. It did not however, become a useful tool for Japan, partly due to shortage of aluminium.

As the Normandy invasion took place Window, dropped with extreme precision by Bomber Command, was used to create non-existent invasion fleets on German radar. Operation Taxable involved Lancasters of No 617 Squadron and Operation Glimmer was flown by Stirlings from No 218 Squadron.

Marshal of the Royal Air Force Sir John Slessor, who had commanded No 5 Group, told the story of an alleged predecessor to Window. Some crews, he said, had convinced themselves that a number of master searchlights covering the Dutch coast, including the Zuider Zee, posed a particular threat to bombers on their outward journey. Rear gunners would therefore carry stocks of empty beer bottles to toss in the areas where the dangerous searchlights were perceived to be and this act was supposed to confuse the radar operating with the searchlights.

There was no scientific evidence to back any of this theory, but Slessor did not want anybody to explain that to his men – he considered that the boost in confidence involved was worth retaining.

Wireless Operator – It was said that you could tell who was a Wireless Operator by looking at boots – the heating duct for cockpits came out by his left foot and it would partly melt the rubber sole of the boot. The Wireless Operator was always roasting, while the rear gunner would be colder than anyone else.

Women's Auxiliary Air Force (WAAF) – Established in June 1939 with the aim of freeing men for operational roles. Its members became known as "WAAFs".

A Women's Royal Air Force had existed briefly at the end of the First World War and at the time of the armistice on November 11 1918 about 25,000 women were serving, many on domestic duties such as cook or orderlies or in administrative trades such as clerks, typists and shorthand writers. A plan to send women overseas was scuppered by the end of hostilities. Originally it was intended that women should be permanently employed in the post First World War RAF, in a range of trades, but economic circumstances led to the scrapping of the plan.

The name Women's Royal Air Force was used again from 1949, when the WAAF was re-formed and, in 1994, the women's service became fully integrated with the RAF.

A WAAF studies a pictorial airfield map.

At the outbreak of the Second World War some senior officers were against placing women in roles traditionally carried out by men, such as in control rooms. The doubters featured supposed lack of stamina and inability to cope under fire, as well as exposure to bad language, amongst their concerns.

By the end of the Battle of Britain one Empire Gallantry Medal (later exchanged for the George Cross) and six Military Medals had been earned by WAAFs in Fighter and Coastal

Commands. In Bomber Command WAAFs served with distinction in a great variety of roles including in operations rooms, parachute packing and driving.

At least one Bomber Command WAAF was smuggled on to an aircraft about to set off by her boyfriend, a member of the crew and took part in a raid. At Scampton Leading Aircraftwoman Iris Price joined the crew of the No 153 Squadron Lancaster, given the name *Vicious Virgin* and flown by a Canadian Flying Officer Bob Purves. The target was a benzol plant at Gelsenkirchen. She survived, despite on the return trip becoming unconscious through lack of oxygen.

WAAFs did not become subject to full military discipline until the passing in 1941 of the Defence (Women's Forces) Regulations.

Some equivalent ranks

WAAF	RAF
Commandant-in-Chief	Air Marshal
Air Chief Commandant	Air Vice-Marshal
Air Commandant	Air Commodore
Group Officer	Group Captain
Wing Officer	Wing Commander
Squadron Officer	Squadron Leader
Flight Officer	Flight Lieutenant
Section Officer	Flying Officer
Assistant Section Officer	Pilot Officer
Senior Sergeant	Flight Sergeant
Sergeant	Sergeant
Corporal	Corporal
Aircraftwoman 1st Class	Aircraftman 1st Class
Aircraftwoman 2nd Class	Aircraftman 2nd Class

POSTSCRIPT

Imperial War Graves Commission
Wooburn House,
Wooburn Green
High Wycombe
Bucks
3 Dec 1945

Dear Sir or Madam

I venture to ask for your assistance in completing the attached form.

The Imperial War Graves Commission have been entrusted, for this war as for the last, with the duty of permanently commemorating those members of His Majesty's Naval, Military and Air Forces from all parts of the British Empire who die in the service of the Allied cause. The Commission will consequently be responsible for marking and caring for the graves, or, in the case of those who have no known grave, for making provision for other suitable form of commemoration, and also for recording all names in permanent Registers. This work will be carried out at the cost of the Commission, whose funds are provided by all the Governments of the Empire.

A headstone of the same simple pattern will, as before, mark each grave; thus every man, rich or poor, General or Private, will be honoured in the same way.

In order to carry out these duties, and to complete the permanent Registers, the Commission desire certain additional information which they hope you will be so good as to supply on the attached form, which should then be returned to the Commission.

You will notice that a space has been left on the form for a personal inscription to be selected by the relatives, if they so desire, for engraving on the headstone. Where, owing to the course of military operations, it has so far been impossible to find or identify a grave, no personal inscription should be inserted on the form. Should the grave eventually be discovered I shall, of course, write to you again and you will then have a further opportunity to choose an inscription.

Some relatives have expressed the wish to pay for this personal inscription, and an opportunity will be given to them later on of meeting the cost. Should they not wish to do so, the cost will be borne by the Commission.

Yours faithfully

Fabian Ware

Vice-Chairman

A letter typical of those received by families at the end of the war.

BIBLIOGRAPHY

Among the books consulted in compiling this Dictionary were:-

A Burford Boy, Sue Shayler, self published, 2007

American Aircraft of World War II, David Mondey, Hamlyn, 1982

B-24 Liberator Units of the Eighth Air Force, Robert F Dorr, Osprey Publishing edition, 1999

Battle under the Moon, Jack Currie, Airdata Publications, 1995

Beyond the Dams to the Tirpitz, Alan Cooper, William Kimber & Co, 1983

Bomber Boys, Patrick Bishop, HarperPress, 2007

Bomber Command, HMSO, 1941

Bomber Command, Max Hastings, Book Club Associates edition, 1980

Bomber Command, 1939-45, Richard Overy, HarperCollins, 1997

Bomber Command Losses of the Second World War, W R Chorley, six volumes from 1992, Midland Counties Publications

Bomber Command Museum Guide, Royal Air Force Museum, undated

Bomber Harris, Dudley Saward, Buchan & Enright, 1984

Bomber Harris, His Life and Times, Henry Probert, Greenhill Books, 2003

Bomber Offensive, Marshal of the Royal Air Force, Sir Arthur Harris, Collins, 1947

Courage and Air Warfare: The Allied Aircrew Experience in the Second World War, Mark K Wells, Frank Cass, 1995.

Day Bomber, Arthur Eyton-Jones, Sutton Publishing 1998

Enemy Coast Ahead, Guy Gibson, Goodall Publications edition, 1986

Footprints in the Sands of Time, Oliver Clutton-Brock, Grub Street, 2003

For Valour, Chaz Bowyer, Grub Street, 1992

Freedom's Battle, Volume 2, The War in the Air 1939-45, Gavin Lyall, Hutchinson, 1968

High Commanders of the Royal Air Force, Air Commodore Henry Probert, HMSO, 1991

Inferno, Keith Lowe, Viking, 2007

Lancaster, Leo McKinstry, John Murray, 2009

Lincolnshire Airfields of the Second World War, Patrick Otter, Countryside Books, 1996

London at War 1939-45, Philip Ziegler, Sinclair-Stevenson, 1995

Men of Air, Kevin Wilson, Weidenfeld & Nicolson, 2007

Missing in Action, Peggy Ryle, W H Allen, 1979

Night Flyer, Lewis Brandon, DSO, DFC, William Kimber, 1961

No Time For Fear, Victor F Gammon, Arms & Armor, 1998

Operation Chastise, John Sweetman, Jane's, 1982

Paths to Freedom, Bob Kellow, edited by Peter Carlyle-Gordge, Kellow Corporation, 1992

RAAF Over Europe, edited by Frank Johnson, Eyre & Spottiswoode, 1946

RAF Squadrons, Wing Commander C G Jefford, 2001

Target Berlin, Jeffrey L Ethell and Alfred Price, Arms and Armour Press edition, 1989

The Bombing Offensive Against Germany, Noble Frankland, Faber, 1965

The Dam Busters, Paul Brickhill, Pan Books edition, 1954

The Oxford Companion to World War ll, I C B Dear and M R D Foot, Encyclopedia.com, 2001

The Right of the Line, John Terraine, Hodder and Stoughton, 1985

The Royal Air Force Volunteer Reserve, Memories, Wing Commander Alex Dickson, Royal Air Force, 1997

The Second World War, Volume ll, Their Finest Hour, Winston S Churchill, Cassell & Co, 1949

The Source Book of the RAF, Ken Delve, Airlife, 1994

The Strategic Air Offensive Against Germany, Sir Charles Webster and Noble Frankland, four volumes, HMSO, 1961

The World Encyclopedia of Bombers, Francis Crosby, Hermes House, 2010

Wellington in Action, Ron Mackay, Squadron/Signal Publications, 1986

We Speak From the Air, HMSO, 1942

Oxford Dictionary of National Biography online

Britain at War, various issues

Everyone's War, various issues

Royal Air Force Historical Society Journal, various issues

National Archive, various files

National Library of Australia – folders MS 10069